Praise for *The Leader*

'If you weren't resilient before, you will be after read this book!'

Dr Rob Hicks, TV doctor, author,
medical consultant

'A must read for any leader looking towards building
personal and team resilience, thought-provoking with lots
of opportunities to stop, pause and reflect. There are lots of
scenarios and practical exercises to stimulate ideas and at the
end of each chapter there is a process to help you identify a
personal action plan. A great additional to add to an existing
leaders tool kit.'

Robert Freund, Head of Learning and Development,
Northamptonshire Healthcare
NHS Foundation Trust

'No better time to assess your resilience and your ability to
lead others when things appear tough. *The Leader's Guide to
Resilience* is the go-to resource for my self-reflection and how
I show up as a leader.'

Peter Priebe, Executive Vice President,
Chief Innovation and Investment Officer, WATG

'A timely, welcome and practical book about resilience, which
provides tools and techniques to build personal strength in an
easy-to-apply manner. Suitable for all levels – from students to
experienced leaders, from individuals to teams – and written
in an energising style; this book motivates you to survive,
rebuild and thrive . . . and gives you the momentum and
guidance to do so.'

Professor Vishanth Weerakkody, Dean,
Faculty of Management, Law and Social Sciences,
University of Bradford

'Everyone from individuals to team leaders would benefit enormously from the lessons propounded within this book's chapters – easy to absorb and assimilate, the practical exercises provided propel readers to delve deep within themselves before proceeding to achieve greater resilience in order to cope with every work situation and all of life's realities.'

Vivienne Lee, Director, Malaysia Airports (Niaga) Sdn. Bhd. (and optional Yin Yoga and Mindfulness Instructor)

'Coaching for resilience has never been more important. This is a great and engaging read, full of brilliant information, theory, models and practical exercises that really deliver results. A truly complimentary and terrific resource for me to share with my clients.'

Martin Turner, Executive Coach

'The ultimate guide to a deep self-audit for personal and professional change, developing authentic self-awareness, Audrey acts as your personal coach, to challenge yourself as an individual, evaluate the impact your actions have on others, and motivate you to forcefully take action to address your learning, build a plan to successfully implement your strategic vision and manage the change. A must-read for those who have little time, are invested in continuous growth in leadership and/or play a part in developing generation NOW and influence the future generation of leaders and decision makers. . . .'

Heather Carr, Project Manager (student and graduate personal development), community coach and mentor, Brunel University London

'At the heart of leadership is a leader's ability to build resilience. Through refreshingly practical and engaging activities, this book shows you how to ADOPT resilience for yourself and your team. *The Leader's Guide to Resilience* is a must-read.'

Dr Daisy Walsh, formerly Head of Engineering, Construction and Computing at Bath College

'Dr Tang has written a terrific book that's accessible and easy to read, making it ideal for busy and overwhelmed leaders in need of support and guidance. The genius of this book is in its practical approach – by providing clear direction and actions to those who need it most. This book is a practical and interactive tool that encourages you to think and act in simple but effective ways that are designed to build resilience. And what a time to have written this book! 2020 may have thrown the world a curveball (or two), but Dr Tang is here to help leaders develop the mental resilience necessary to respond and thrive.'

Christina LaMarca, Head of Marketing and Events, Energy Intelligence

'Skilfully and seamlessly weaving together the theory with thought-provoking practical exercises, this inspirational triumph is the go-to resource for any leader seeking to arm themselves with the resilience to thrive.'

Natasha Jones, Partner, Laceys Solicitors

'Experienced in coaching and public speaking, Audrey vibrantly brings the written word to life with her compassionate yet uncompromising challenge to the reader "to be flexible, to adapt . . . to truly know your own mind".'

Suman Lodh, Senior Lecturer in Finance, Departmental Research Leader, Middlesex University

The Leader's Guide to Resilience

Pearson

At Pearson, we believe in learning – all kinds of learning for all kinds of people. Whether it's at home, in the classroom or in the workplace, learning is the key to improving our life chances.

That's why we're working with leading authors to bring you the latest thinking and best practices, so you can get better at the things that are important to you. You can learn on the page or on the move, and with content that's always crafted to help you understand quickly and apply what you've learned.

If you want to upgrade your personal skills or accelerate your career, become a more effective leader or more powerful communicator, discover new opportunities or simply find more inspiration, we can help you make progress in your work and life.

Every day our work helps learning flourish, and wherever learning flourishes, so do people.

To learn more, please visit us at **www.pearson.com/uk**

The Financial Times

With a worldwide network of highly respected journalists, *The Financial Times* provides global business news, insightful opinion and expert analysis of business, finance and politics. With over 500 journalists reporting from 50 countries worldwide, our in-depth coverage of international news is objectively reported and analysed from an independent, global perspective.

To find out more, visit **www.ft.com**

The Leader's Guide to Resilience

How to use soft skills to
get hard results

Audrey Tang

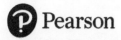 Pearson

Harlow, England • London • New York • Boston • San Francisco • Toronto • Sydney • Dubai • Singapore • Hong Kong
Tokyo • Seoul • Taipei • New Delhi • Cape Town • São Paulo • Mexico City • Madrid • Amsterdam • Munich • Paris • Milan

PEARSON EDUCATION LIMITED

KAO Two
KAO Park
Harlow CM17 9SR
United Kingdom
Tel: +44 (0)1279 623623
Web: **www.pearson.com/uk**

First edition published 2021 (print and electronic)

ISBN: 978-1-292-33129-4 (print)
         978-1-292-33128-7 (PDF)
         978-1-292-33127-0 (ePub)

British Library Cataloguing-in-Publication Data
A catalogue record for the print edition is available from the British Library

Library of Congress Cataloging-in-Publication Data
Names: Tang, Audrey, author.
Title: The leader's guide to resilience : how to use soft skills to get
    hard results / Audrey Tang.
Description: First editoin. | New York : Pearson, 2021. | Series: The
    leader's guide | Includes bibliographical references and index.
Identifiers: LCCN 2020040473 (print) | LCCN 2020040474 (ebook) | ISBN
    9781292331294 (paperback) | ISBN 9781292331287 (pdf) | ISBN
    9781292331270 (epub)
Subjects: LCSH: Leadership. | Organizational resilience. | Teams in the
    workplace.
Classification: LCC HD57.7 .T365 2021 (print) | LCC HD57.7 (ebook) | DDC
    658.4/092—dc23
LC record available at https://lccn.loc.gov/2020040473
LC ebook record available at https://lccn.loc.gov/2020040474

10 9 8 7 6 5 4 3 2 1
25 24 23 22 21

Cover design by Michelle Morgan At the Pop Ltd
Print edition typeset in Melior LT Std 9/13 by SPi Global

NOTE THAT ANY PAGE CROSS REFERENCES REFER TO THE PRINT EDITION

Contents

About the author

Audrey is a chartered psychologist (CPsychol), and author
of *The Leader's Guide to Mindfulness* (Pearson, 2018) and
Be A Great Manager Now! (Pearson, 2016 and Book of
the Month in WHSmith Travel Stores). She is a presenter
and wellness advocate fronting 'Psych Back to Basics' on
Disruptive LIVE, a YouTube channel, and is the resident
psychologist on *The Chrissy B Show* – the UK's only TV
programme dedicated to mental health and wellbeing.
She also offers expert comment as a psychologist through TV,
radio and published media, and broadcasts her own podcast
'Retrain Your Brain for Success'. She speaks at national
and international conferences in the fields of resilience,
leadership and team cohesion, is a CPD-accredited trainer
and FIRO-B profiler, and regularly consults and hosts
webinars and lectures offering applied psychology and
practical coaching for personal and professional success.

Publisher's acknowledgements

16 Emerald Publishing Limited: O'Connor CA (1993), "Resistance: The Repercussions of Change", Leadership & Organization Development Journal, Vol. 14 No. 6, pp. 30–36. https://doi.org/10.1108/01437739310145615 **17 Mary Ann Liebert, Inc:** O'Leary V.E. & Ickovics J.R. (1995) Resilience and thriving in response to challenge: An opportunity for a paradigm shift in women's health. Women's Health: Research on Gender, Behavior, and Policy, 1(2), 121–142 **13 A.A. Milne:** Quoted by A.A. Milne **8 The Wellbeing Project:** The Wellbeing Project, The 5 PILLARS OF RESILIENCE, https://thewellbeingproject.co.uk/wp-content/uploads/2017/12/The-5-Pillars-FacGuide-TTT-MASTER-2017-1.pdf **8 Dr. Arielle Schwartz:** Arielle Schwartz, 6 Pillars of Resilience, https://drarielleschwartz.com/6-pillars-of-resilience-dr-arielle-schwartz/#.Xw1nfCgzbDc **35 MAHLE Powertrain Ltd:** Sanderson D (2019) Talk on Mahle-Powertrain capabilities, May 2020 www.mahle-powertrain.com/capabilities (accessed May 2020) **36 William Shakespeare:** Shakespeare's Henry V, Act-III, Scene-I **37 HarperCollins:** Peter L.J. & Hull R. The Peter Principle, William Morrow & Co Inc, 1969 (Pan Books edition 1970) **58 G.M. Hill Co:** Baum, L.F., & Denslow, W.W. (1900). The wonderful wizard of Oz. Chicago: G.M. Hill Co. **80 William Shakespeare:** Lady Macbeth, William Shakespeare Act1 sc5 **81 John Cleese:** Quoted by John Cleese **82 Universal Pictures:** James Hunt to Niki Lauda, Rush **82 Surviving Leadership:** Faulkner M. (2018) Surviving Leadership Blog https://survivingleadership.blog/2018/07/31/the-power-and-danger-of-being-liked/

(accessed May 2020) **91 D. McKay Company, Incorporated:** Bloom B.S., Engelhart M.D., Furst E.J., Hill W.H., Krathwohl D.R. (1956) Taxonomy of educational objectives: The classification of educational goals. Handbook I: Cognitive domain. New York: David McKay Company **108 Allandale Online Publishing:** Tzu S. (1910) The Art of War https://sites. ualberta.ca/~enoch/Readings/The_Art_Of_War.pdf (accessed May 2020) **108 Pearson Education:** C.K. Seet, 1951 cited by Tang A. (2017) The Leader's Guide to Mindfulness, Pearson & FT **125 Arlie Russell Hochschild:** Quoted by Arlie Russell Hochschild **126 Arlie Russell Hochschild:** Quoted by Arlie Russell Hochschild **154 Pearson Education:** David A. Kolb, Experiential Learning: Experience as the Source of Learning and Development, 1984, Prentice-Hall. **154 Harvard Business School Publishing:** Argryis **159 Centre of Excellence:** Centre for Excellence (2018) Dialectic Behaviour Therapy Diploma, Course Notes **161 William Butler Yeats:** Yeats W.B. (c1899) Aedh Wishes for the Cloths of Heaven https:// www.oneirishrover.com/poem-yeats-wishes-cloths-heaven/ (accessed May 2020) **161 John Goldwyn:** The Chrissy B Show (2018), The Chrissy B Show, Sky 191, UCKG **166 National Public Radio, Inc:** Thunberg G. (2019) UN Climate Change Summit https://www.npr.org/2019/09/23/763452863/ transcript-greta-thunbergs-speech-at-the-u-n-climate-action-summit (accessed May 2020) **168 National Public Radio, Inc:** Thunberg G. (2019) UN Climate Change Summit https://www.npr.org/2019/09/23/763452863/ transcript-greta-thunbergs-speech-at-the-u-n-climate-action-summit (accessed May 2020) **168 Girlguiding UK:** Girlguiding UK (2020) Website https://www.girlguiding. org.uk/ (accessed May 2020) **169 MANSUETO VENTURES:** Blakely L. (2018) Patagonia's Unapologetically Political Strategy and the Massive Business it has Built, Inc.com https://www.inc.com/lindsay-blakely/patagonia-2018-company-of-the-year-nominee.html (accessed May 2020)

169 Patagonia, Inc: Patagonia (2020), Website https://www.
patagonia.com/company-info.html (accessed May 2020)
170 BioMed Central: Smith E., Haustein S., Mongeo, P. (2017)
Knowledge sharing in global health research – the impact,
uptake and cost of open access to scholarly literature.
Health Res Policy Sys 15, 73 https://doi.org/10.1186/
s12961-017-0235-3 **170 Medpagetoday:** Medpagetoday Blog
(2018) Website https://www.medpagetoday.com/blogs/
revolutionandrevelation/72407 (accessed May 2020)
170 Springer Nature: Brosch T., Stussi Y., Desrichard O. (2018)
Not my future? Core values and the neural representation
of future events. Cogn Affect Behav Neurosci 18, 476–484
https://doi.org/10.3758/s13415-018-0581-9 **170 Guardian
News & Media Limited:** Watson B. (2016), The troubling
evolution of corporate greenwashing, The Guardian https://
www.theguardian.com/sustainable-business/2016/aug/20/
greenwashing-environmentalism-lies-companies (accessed
May 2020) **174 Harvard Business Publishing:** Daimler M. (2018)
Why Great Employees Leave Great Cultures, HBR.org https://
hbr.org/2018/05/why-great-employees-leave-great-cultures
(accessed May 2020) **175 BCA Green Mark:** BCA Greenmark
(2018) Document https://www.bca.gov.sg/GreenMark/others/
GM_HW_2018_Pilot.pdf (accessed May 2020) **179 Carl Jung:**
Quoted by Carl Jung **181 The Xenon Group:** 7 key pieces of
sustainability related legislation that you should be aware of,
Xenon Group, 2018 **198 Mcgraw Hill Education:** Spears S.
(2009) The High Velocity Edge, Mcgraw Hill **211 Christopher
Bollas:** Quoted by Christopher Bollas **225 Jasmine O'Dell:**
O'Dell J. (2020) Poetry in Isolation "Jasmine O'Dell, @
poetryinisolation (Instagram)" (accessed May 2020) **229
Welcome Break:** Rodgers C., Marshall N. (2020) Welcome
Break International Women's Day Event, Newport Pagnell
233 Hachette Filipacchi Médias: Cauldwell T (1983) A pillar
of iron, Mass Market Paperback **238 The Atlantic Monthly
Group:** Lewis H. (2020) How Panic Buying Revealed the

Problem With the Modern World The Atlantic https://amp-theatlantic-com.cdn.ampproject.org/v/s/amp.theatlantic.com/amp/article/608731/?amp_js_v=a3&_gsa=1&usqp=mq331AQFKAGwASA%3D#referrer=https%3A%2F%2Fwww.google.com&_tf=From%20%251%24s&ampshare=https%3A%2F%2Fwww.theatlantic.com%2Finternational%2Farchive%2F2020%2F03%2Fcoronavirus-panic-buying-britain-us-shopping%2F608731%2F (accessed May 2020) **26 Alamy Stock Photo:** Chronicle of World History/Alamy Stock Photo

Foreword

John Goldwyn, Senior Vice President – London, WATG

Today, as I sit here, writing, the world is locked away at home. We are isolated and existing alone, or in our family groups, to protect our health services who, in turn, are protecting us and our loved ones from a global pandemic. I am lucky enough to be spending precious time with my family while the world spins on its new and unsettling axis. When September 11, 2001 occurred, we could see our enemy – or at least imagine one. The Coronavirus has been a global nuclear explosion that we can't see or hear. We have little idea what this means for humanity, let alone our own daily lives. However, it is important that the hard lessons learned at these extreme times are taken forward as our daily life re-emerges.

As a landscape architect and master planner, people and places are in my DNA. Resilience is a part of design in everything I do. Resilience is about preparation for, and recovering from, shocks. This can be applied to the self, the business, the city. Such events can be anticipated events or *black swans*. Resilience can be locked into design to allow for all eventualities. This does not always have to be technically complex. For example, food security is a global issue. On a local scale – urban orchards, allotments, edible gardens and rooftop beehives – we can start to address the problem. These are small steps, but we must start somewhere. Cultivation and gardening is also a pursuit that nurtures good mental health. Parks are such a valuable place for people to express themselves in multiple ways, from obsessional jogging and cycling to just relaxing. As human beings, our natural state is a social one. People deeply crave togetherness. As formal spirituality wanes in western society, we look to public meeting places in cities to socialise, share and connect. Like the cities of which I speak, we must ensure that we design resilience into our daily lives. This is a book that can help you and me to do just that.

Health experts suggest that anxiety can be triggered by feeling unable to control your future. So, in my own life, I focus on the small things I can control to achieve the ecological ideals I passionately believe in. Of course, I recycle and re-use. I have stopped flying, but that's a long story. I rarely drive my car. I cycle daily to my office in central London. I compost food scraps and other waste in my wormery to feed the plants that I cultivate in my tiny urban garden. I have adopted a largely plant-based diet. I would grow more food, like my mum does, if I had just a little more space! I always select plant species that attract pollinators and paving materials that absorb water. And I enjoy the outdoor space that my garden creates for some mindful relaxation. As Winnie the Pooh said: '*Sometimes I sits and thinks, and sometimes I just sits*'. I live for long, wild swims in cold, open water – as much for my mental health as for the physical benefits. I truly believe that being 'in' nature is an incredibly important mindful therapy. A connection with nature is extremely comforting and reassuring to me. Like the *little things* that I do with my daily life, it is surprisingly easy to change your life by using the small steps to which Audrey refers in this book, to instil mental resilience.

My design team consists of people from myriad backgrounds and cultures. We share a core desire to enhance the quality of human life. We believe in preservation, and that new ideas can underpin old ones; celebrating and honouring magnificent landscapes rather than removing or replacing them. Stories in the land, and history as witnessed by ancestral trees, are measured in centuries or millennia, not our own lifetimes. On looking at the degradation of our planet, we aspire to design in a way that aligns with the intelligence of the natural world. Nature is always smarter than us and often the resilience we seek is embedded within natural systems rather than complex engineered solutions. One of our current concepts is about retro-fitting parkets and gardens into cities without changing existing infrastructure. Our goal is to add urban resilience into the places that we already use and love. This lies in the form of vegetated façades and planting corridors that will clean the air, help to reduce flooding and cool the streets in summer. But crucially, they will also provide much-needed spaces for people to socialise, express themselves or just 'be'. In the same way as I look to make cities more resilient, this book will help you to 'retro fit' resilience into your mindset and daily life. Most of us probably do not have a 'master plan' for ourselves. If we survey our lives, in the way that I use maps to understand sites, then maybe we can recognise what needs to change and make steps to go about doing it. As we learn to listen to ourselves (as a designer I listen to nature), we will start to understand what really matters to each of us.

Flashing back to 2018, I had the privilege of meeting Audrey in Athens where we were both speakers at the Global Megatrends conference. I can safely say that she outshone me substantially on the lectern; however, I held my own when it came to pop culture, video games and music from our childhood! We discovered shared values and we are now good friends. And Audrey has since helped me address my public speaking deficiencies with some withering analysis and agonising theatrical vocal exercises.

Since this meeting, we have stretched our research and thought processes to engage on design projects to address psychology and mindfulness and my team now incorporates other global scientific experts to better understand how our work links to local custom. Not only are we thinking about how to design to conserve and enhance both the natural and built environment, we're also thinking about what that experience does for the mind and soul.

When design work speaks vividly and with great respect to nature, it can benefit from local intelligence gathered over centuries. As the world shifts and presents us with new challenges, we see an emerging purpose – to ensure that people and the environments they work and live in can truly thrive. In parallel, we already build resilience into our daily lives by 'downing tools', having a walk or enjoying a cup of tea during a stressful day. As you read this book, you will start to recognise these strategies, and augment them with others that are often not 'work related'. Contained in the following pages are devices that will help us to emerge better equipped to deal with our own personal environment within which we can start to thrive.

About John

John Goldwyn leads the planning and landscape studio in WATG's London office, and brings a broad variety of global project experience to the team. His design responds first to the place and the site – looking for the stories in the land. He is committed to finding sustainable solutions for clients that balance economic, social and environmental factors. John believes that the commercial success of any project is directly related to its design content.

For more information: **london@watg.com**

Introduction

This book was commissioned because there is a need for it in leadership. It was finished during the 2020 Global Pandemic when resilience proved essential – and never too late to build.

The world is ever challenging. It is moving at an increasingly fast pace; environmental and social issues are faced daily, and successful organisations need a means to navigate the storm, ride the waves, survive and grow.

As a development trainer and coach I teach resilience for high performance and leadership success regularly, not just because I see value in the subject, but because I see what you can potentially become if you apply the principles in your everyday life.

This book offers exactly that: easy-to-action tips and strategies rooted in theory and effective in practice to help you, your teams and your organisations withstand the surrounding pressures, and continue to grow.

Resilience is commonly understood to mean a person's ability to withstand hardship. It might also imply praise for their mental fortitude or describe their refusal to capitulate under pressure. The word derives from the Latin *resiliens*, meaning 'to rebound, recoil', i.e. from *re-* 'back' (see re-) + *salire* 'to jump, leap' (Back jump/'bounce back' is the closest common phrase). It has permeated many schools of thought being defined as:

- to '. . . demonstrate both strength and flexibility . . . while displaying minimal dysfunctional behaviour' (O'Connor, 1993: Organisational change management);

- '. . . the ability to bounce back and withstand hardship by repairing oneself', and to '. . . recover and become stronger . . .' (Henderson and Milstein, 1996; Higgins, 1994; Wolin and Wolin, 1993: Psychology and Social Science);

- to '. . . withstand or successfully cope with adversity' and to '. . . survive stress and rise above' (Rutter, 1979; Werner and Smith, 2001: Development);

- '. . . to recognise pain, acknowledge its purpose, tolerate it . . .' (O'Leary and Ickovics, 1995: Medicine);

- A means whereby large groups or communities can be structured so as to withstand adversity as an integrated whole (Fleming and Ledogar, 2008: Resilient cities and communities).

A simplistic model comes from Nishikawa (2006) who conceptualises Resilience as having three components:

- Survival

- Recovery

- Thriving.

This book uses that as a starting point, but develops it as follows: Resilience is about being able to navigate three dips – through which one must survive, recover (or rebuild) and thrive:

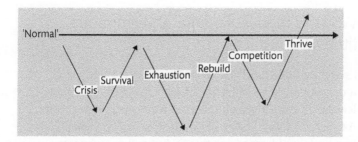

. . . and the only way to do that is to build the fitness beforehand. It's like physical fitness – resilience is not about the final test, it is about preparing for it long before you need to prove your worth.

Further, a different mental and emotional stamina is needed to buffer each dip.

In the period of crisis, to survive one must be able to be flexible, to adapt, to collaborate, to learn new skills. To recover from exhaustion and rebuild one must have faith. That means having the strength in yourself to keep going, even when you are weighed down. It means knowing that you can do it, because you have to, and continuing even if you no longer have support. Finally, in order to grow you face competition, envy, treachery – you must remain focused. You must be able to navigate the white noise of people who have their own agendas or may be trying to force you in directions that they think are right – but are not . . . if you know your own mind.

The psychological challenges are different at each point, but the message remains the same . . . you need to keep flexing your energy muscles so you can cope.

Therefore this book offers you accessible methods to **survive** the challenges you – and your teams – may be facing both professionally and personally, as well as means to **recover**, rebuild and strengthen your resources to not only withstand and rebound from adversity, but actually **grow**.

Why this model of mental and emotional fitness?

I started writing this book at the end of 2019, I completed it during the global pandemic of 2020. In 'social distancing lockdown' I experienced first-hand what went on in a crisis. As I am not a frontline or key worker, I wasn't personally involved; but I learned one thing – it was those who were emotionally and mentally fit that coped best.

And it wasn't because you needed that strength to survive. As I conclude at the end of Part 2 – 'Crisis' is often the *known* enemy. While it doesn't hurt to have your energy tank topped up, survival in the crisis period is helped by adrenaline. The bigger the crisis, the more the support that is rallied as the community pulls together. The hardest slog comes when the crisis is conquered.

After the storm is the calm, that is the hardest part of all. Those in the frontline are exhausted. There is devastation in the form of debt, despair, loss and trauma, and compassion is now running dry. You need to pick up again when there is less camaraderie, less charity and even more fear of 'now what?'

Then, when things are normalised, you have a third spurt – the chance to thrive.

How this book works

Part 1 focuses on you, offering you ways to survive, recover and grow when faced with challenge, and also growth – when the opportunity presents.

Part 2 supports you in establishing the principles of the resilience – and thriving – mindset within your organisation and *system-wide*, i.e. within the broader community in which you function.

The Epilogue then reflects how to maintain that momentum, especially within a world sometimes beset with uncertainty and fear.

You may have read my previous book, *The Leader's Guide to Mindfulness*. The focus of that book was to support you to better manage your life as it is, through deepening your awareness of your world, and the tools at your disposal to interact with it. *The Leader's Guide to Resilience* will help you change it – should you desire. Resilience is about challenge and change – it is not about simply returning to the start, but moving forward into a new future, while learning from the past. Further, if you have been fortunate enough not to have had upheaval imposed on you, you may choose to grow through seeking challenges yourself. Mindfulness will calm you; resilience will arm you.

And arm you it must, because building resilience is about taking action. Mindfulness will raise your awareness, but then what do you do? Awareness is not enough – beyond it *must come action* or you will be the most enlightened person who never lived.

Taking action

With this in mind, you will be presented with ideas or actions that may differ from your usual practice, and you are encouraged to reflect on this variety of behaviour options. There will be reflection points, questions to ask of yourself, of your teams and of your organisational functioning. You will be given suggestions to build your personal, professional and organisational strength, and exercises to identify areas of weaknesses to be addressed. Building strength is not easy – but it will be worth it.

Your 'end-of-chapter toolkit'

ADOPT Resilience now

At the end of each chapter a practical exercise or tip following my ADOPT model will help you continue to practise and embed what has been learned. Consider trying it right now!

> **ADOPT**:
>
> **A**ct
>
> **D**eal

Optimise

Prepare

Thrive

Act: Be pro-active rather than letting life live you. Know that you always have the power of choice. Not only can you *own* your narrative (no matter what it is), but you can *write* it; however, you have to pick up the pen! Habit, whether conscious or unconscious, and no matter how it came to be, can prevent this. Therefore, sometimes one of the most impactful things you can do in an emotional, mental or physical impasse is *something*! Anything – and always *something different to habit*. Even in the direst situation, one outcome is likely; so what stops you from trying something different to swing the pendulum in your favour? On a smaller scale, what holds us back are the boundaries (often assumptions) we place on ourselves – how do we *know* someone won't like something or that something will go wrong? Why not be pro-active and find out?

> *This week*: If you find yourself going around in circles on something, mix it up, try something a little different to the norm, even if it is simply just stopping if you would normally race into battle.

Deal: Procrastination is not always helpful. A considered delay might be, but often it is more effective to deal with minor issues while they remain such.

> *This week:* If there is one thing you have been putting off, do it.

Optimise: Look after your physical and mental wellness so that you are fit enough to face whatever life throws at you. *And* make the most of everything you *do* choose to do. Unfortunately caring for others does not excuse you from caring for yourself. If you have additional duties, try and make sure you energise yourself in the most productive

manner for you. As I recharge like an extravert, I am
energised when I spend time with friends and family whom
I love. If you recharge like an introvert, get that 'alone time',
even if it is a quick walk or a moment to simply breathe.
AND, if you are going to spend quality time with a loved one,
don't dilute it by using your phone at the same time. If you
are going to rebuild something from scratch, reflect on what
went wrong and input ways of making it better. Optimising
your work and play can bring you greater fulfilment – and
even greater positive results: when I'm energised I work
better too!

> *This week:* Whatever you choose to do, get the most out of it that
> you can. If this means curating your choices of who you spend
> time with and what you do, so be it! I am also keeping a 'wellness
> pledge photo album'. My pledge is to do things which energise me
> and capturing the photos enables me to look back at them and
> smile if I need an extra boost. It's a very happy album! Try it!

Prepare: Always aim for excellence (rather than 'perfection',
which is subjective). While I often advocate a positive
approach, there are times when it is important to have a 'plan
B' (or C, D, E . . . Z). Don't plan *for* things to go wrong, but
rather be mindful of the options in case they do, and make
sure you've covered your bases as best you can beforehand.

> *This week:* Take an extra moment to double check that email or
> document that you are going to send off.

Thrive: It's not just about getting by – it's about *flourishing*!
Resilience is not just about building healthy practices before,
and to hold back, the point of crisis; it is about planting the
seeds so you can *bloom*. This means that it is important to
surround yourself with things and people that nurture your
strength and allow – and encourage – you to grow.

This week: Practise gratitude as a form of editing your life. Make a note of three things/people you are grateful for each day, and at the end of the week be mindful of what comes up regularly. Spend more time nurturing those elements of your life. This act of nurture may also energise you to better manage the duties and responsibilities which are more routine, with just that little bit more flair (and optimisation!!) – after all, 'duty' was probably at some point a wished-for priority!

These five simple ways help build your resilience and choose healthy responses *before the point of crisis*. It doesn't mean crises won't happen, but ADOPT Resilience as part of your routine and you will feel better placed to survive, recover and thrive. Emotional and mental fitness is the same as physical fitness, it needs to be exercised, and the best time is when it is easy to do so.

Some things in this book will work first time and they may become your 'go-to' practices; others might not, but that doesn't mean they won't in future, and some you may choose to adapt to a way that suits you. This is all ok – it means you are always actively and reflectively building and testing your strengths.

Resilience and thriving begin not with disregard of what may have caused us pain or distress, but with acceptance and learning. Do not 'forget who you were', but learn that if circumstances have changed, the strategies and behaviours which have served you well in the past, may no longer be as effective. Yes, they form the basis of your grit to survive, but make room for the new so you can begin to live. Don't depose – transform. Don't replace – revive. You have always been enough, but you have the potential to be more – there is no upper limit.

Therefore, all the way through, irrespective of whether you are learning to survive, build, recover, strengthen, withstand or cope, this book will also offer you ways in which you can **thrive**.

Resilience is not new – it is not something you need to add; it is already within you. It may need to be uncovered, nurtured, or perhaps restored, but its potential is in all of us.

Are you ready to grow?

References

Fleming, J. and Ledogar, R. J. (2008) Resilience, an evolving concept: A review of literature relevant to Aboriginal research. *Pimatisiwin*, Vol. 6, No. 2, 7–23.

Henderson, N. and Milstein, M. M. (1996) *Resiliency in Schools: Making It Happen for Students and Educators*. Corwin Press.

Higgins, G. O. (1994) *Resilient Adults: Overcoming a cruel past*. Jossey-Bass.

Nishikawa, Y. (2006) *Thriving in the Face of Adversity: Perceptions of elementary-school principals*. University of La Verne, CA.

O'Connor, C. A. (1993) Resistance: The repercussions of change. *Leadership & Organization Development Journal*, Vol. 14, No. 6, 30–36 https://doi.org/10.1108/01437739310145615

O'Leary, V. E. and Ickovics, J. R. (1995) Resilience and thriving in response to challenge: An opportunity for a paradigm shift in women's health. *Women's Health*, Vol. 1, No. 2, 121–142.

Rutter, M. (1979) Protective factors in children's responses to stress and disadvantage. In M. W. Kent and J. E. Rolf (eds)

Primary Prevention of Psychopathology: Social competence in children (Vol. 3, pp. 49–74). University Press of New England.

Werner, E. E. and Smith, R. S. (2001) *Journeys from Childhood to Midlife: Risk resilience and recovery.* Cornell University Press.

Wolin, S. J. and Wolin, S. (1993) *The Resilient Self: How survivors of troubled families rise above adversity.* Villard Books.

part 1

Becoming resilient

Build resilient people

Respond ALWAYS - SOMETIMES - NEVER

Do you:

- Avoid conflict whenever possible?
- Find it hard to set boundaries?
- Attempt only what you know you will succeed at?
- Feel most comfortable when in a relationship?
- Always forgive others, even when you are still hurt by their actions?
- Think you are taken advantage of/treated like a 'doormat'?
- Prioritise the needs of others before your own?

(People Pleaser Quiz adapted from Psychologica.co)

If you said 'ALWAYS' most often, you tend to put the needs of others before those of your own. You may even feel more comfortable doing so, or base your happiness on theirs; for example, 'If they are happy I'm happy'.

If you said 'SOMETIMES' most often, you may be more balanced in your interactions with others – giving and taking as you wish the relationships to allow.

➤

If you said 'NEVER' most often, you may be very focused on protecting your needs and emotions (and therefore may be most in need of this chapter, although it's a useful reminder for those on 'ALWAYS' or 'SOMETIMES').

While a short quiz is no substitute for a formal assessment, this simple thought exercise encourages a greater awareness of how you perceive yourself within your world. The answers are not binding, fixed nor predictive, but if you have such a low sense of self that you most often try to please others, or so great that you seek mainly to please yourself, this is not effective for building resilience.

One of the responses to the self-compassion approach of *The Leader's Guide to Mindfulness* was a question mark over whether mindfulness made one 'selfish'. My perspective is always no. Mindful meditation was originally employed to raise awareness of the self so that you could live better, which in turn meant you would make a more effective (positive) impact on those around you. Through affixing your mask first, you can help others more readily. Resilience starts from the same foundation. Build the self and those around you will likely benefit.

Therefore, this chapter will teach you to be self-ish.

There's no need to be 'hard to get' if you are 'hard to earn'

That is not to say you need to be:

self-important

self-serving

self-sabotaging

self-destructive

. . . nor indeed 'selfish' as the term is commonly used.

Being self-*ish* means you need to think about your behaviours, your choices and your needs, because unless you are aware of, and to some extent can exert power over them – you will only ever be responsive to things that happen to you (too low a sense of self), OR isolate the people who might have been your greatest allies (too great a sense of self). Neither of these outcomes will lead to healthy choices, especially when faced with challenge. In the former case your own contribution is so negated that you yourself can become a burden to those you are trying to support, and in the latter you may find you have alienated the people who could have benefitted from your input.

The importance of being self-ish is that only through a *balance of self-knowledge, how you interact with your world, and mastery over your choices (with awareness of consequence)* can resilience be achieved. Through casting a lens on, and *improving* the actions of your *self,* you are better able to:

▌ understand and assert your value within a situation and be most likely to contribute to the solution;

▌ form healthy collaborations which meet your needs and those of your wider community and which are long-lasting and supportive;

▌ grow.

Resilience roots within a healthy sense of self

The development of a healthy self-awareness and a sense of self occurs through childhood. Children learn, through their experiences within their environment to trust, develop autonomy, take initiative, become industrious, form their identity, engage in intimacy, generate productively and live with integrity (Erikson, 1958, 1963). Unfortunately, if the child does not establish that firm sense of who they are, their behaviours may become those of mistrust, doubt and avoidance of shame, guilt and fear, inferiority, role confusion, isolation, stagnation and despair (Erikson, 1958, 1963). Too weak a sense of self can result in the belief that everyone knows better than you and instead of engaging with your own potential you become an unquestioning drone (likely becoming more and more unhappy with your life); if your sense of self is too much, people may perceive this as arrogance, and find this to be distasteful. Even when surrounded with others who may have a well-developed sense of self, askewed (i.e. self-serving or self-destructive) behaviour can affect the group. Resilience means striking a balance – being self-ish (self-focused or self-aware enough to contribute with purpose and fulfilment – to the best of your ability), *because* of the knowledge that you belong to a wider community.

Without being self-*ish*, unpleasant and unproductive behaviours (e.g. self-sabotage, self-centredness, self-servance or self-destruction) may occur. That is also when those around you may suffer collaterally. Yet, show yourself compassion, devote time to identify and nurture what is important to your personal effectiveness, and you will be stronger, and this will enable you to be strong for others.

Becoming resilient: What builds you up?

The foundations of resilience are often presented in the form of pillars:

What are yours?

Identify up to six things that keep you going, especially through challenge.

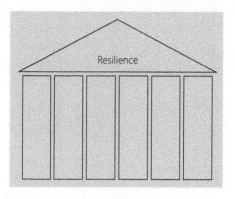

Many writers have looked at theirs:

The Defense Logistics Agency proposes four: Mental health, Physical health, Social health, Spiritual health.

The Wellbeing Project suggests five: Energy, Future focus, Inner drive, Flexible thinking, Strong relationships ... as does 'Bounce Back': Self-care, Self-awareness, Mindfulness, Relationships, Purpose.

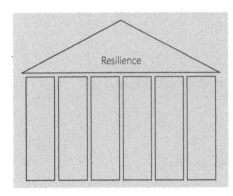

Dr Arielle Schwartz offers six: Growth mindset, Emotional Intelligence, Community connections, Self-expression, Embodiment, Choice & control

... so does EQ Works: Satisfaction with lifestyle, Supportive relationships, Physical Wellbeing, Solution-focused coping, Emotion-focused coping, Positive beliefs.

Knowing what keeps your 'temple' standing will be essential not only for being able to thrive by pushing boundaries or reaching upwards in 'normality', but for rebuilding and surviving when things get difficult. This is applicable on the large, as well as small scale: even if you need the motivation to achieve a small goal, attending to one of your 'pillars' may energise you enough to keep going.

Try this

Write out the pillars which are significant to your ability to succeed, and shade in how plentiful that resource is at the moment. Then, if any pillars are lacking, find a way to fill or replenish them. Do the same with your teams too – and you can also do this for your organisation as a whole:

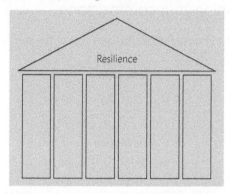

Resilience

What you may find is that when you suddenly attend to 'pillars' that have been neglected previously, the relationship that you have with them may have changed when you weren't looking. For example, if your family is a source (or pillar) of strength, but you haven't spent as much time with them – remember they will still have continued to grow, and you struggle to pick up again where you left off. Use the NLP (neuro-linguistic programming) technique of 'match, pace, lead' for reforming the bonds:

▎ Observe the situation for what it is (match)

▎ Ask to join in with what they are doing (pace alongside – for as long as it takes to be comfortable again)

▎ Then invite them to do something with you (lead).

This technique can be scaled up further to community groups or wider networks you wish to collaborate with. It's not always about enforcing your step onto them – it often works best to take a measured approach.

➤

> Then reflect on the same exercise in a couple of weeks – what improved and how? Reflection is key to recognising that goal achievement is the **start** not the end. Once things are normalised, why stop at 'maintenance'?

In order to grow after your pillars are strong, keep pushing your comfort zone

Another notable model of resilience is that of the comfort zone.

Panic zone
Stretch zone
Comfort zone

When simply going about your daily life, you are often in the 'comfort zone'. When you try a new skill, or undertake a challenge, it may push you into the stretch zone, and when things get tricky very fast or unexpectedly it may mean you fall into the panic zone. Psychologically, as the 'panic zone' is not a pleasant state to be in, understandably you may prefer to avoid it. But testing yourself, especially when the challenge is not essential to your survival, is a good opportunity to check on your resilience when you don't *need* it.

As a leader (and subsequently you may do so for your teams) challenge yourself to move beyond your comfort zone on a regular basis into a stretch zone, and tap into what might lie beyond – the 'panic' zone. For example, perhaps it is 'comfortable' for you to develop yourself and form partnerships. It may be a stretch for you to agree on a common agenda for that partnership, and a 'panic' for you to allow those partnerships to take a leading role, but by taking small steps regularly your 'stretch zone' becomes your new comfort zone.

> **Try this**
>
> Regularly do little things which push you outside your comfort zone, even as simple as ordering a different drink, or upping the ante within a hobby. Even if you have to do these things alone, remember that if you master them, you can then help others who may be afraid.
>
> Building up little acts that broaden your world makes it easier to face – or even take up – a bigger challenge later on.

> *This week:* Undertake a challenge – you don't even need to tell anyone you are doing it (yet). But perhaps it's something you never thought you would do, or you longed for, or perhaps it is even on your 'bucket list'.

Once you are comfortable again, encourage others through talking about your efforts (and struggles!) as well as celebrating your achievements.

Incorporate a 'resilience-based' lifestyle: McEwen's R@W Sustain Model

Kathryn McEwen's R@W Sustain Model is a seven-step elaboration of the process of resilience that can be maintained long term.

1. Recognise your personal values (focus on the self).

2. Align with organisational core values. (That is, make sure you are living your values every day. This is easier to

curate when in a position of leadership, and helpful to be aware of when deciding to remain within a team. Further it can bring a sense of focus to your longer term goals.)

3. Maintain a positive perspective and work through setbacks (easier when you believe in what you are aiming for – i.e. if the organisation's values are in line with yours).

4. Manage stressors as common practice (as with point 3).

5. Establish interaction and co-operation as the norm rather than competition. (When you are living your values, and they are broadly in line with those of your organisation (or community), you are likely to attract similar-minded people to your team. This will be discussed in more detail in Chapter 3.)

6. Maintain mental and physical health (something still sometimes overlooked in organisations with a preference in some areas to allow people to be 'signed off sick' rather than establishing clear support networks).

7. Develop your wider network successfully. (A simple example is, while it may be community minded to source locally, the local source must be *capable* of producing what is needed so they must sometimes be trained or mentored, supported and sometimes even financed. How can the resilient leader ensure a return on their wider investment? . . . Again awareness of and connection to the overall vision can help.)

The key to this model is to recognise your values – *and live them regularly*. If what you value is out of synchronicity with what you are doing, this leads to great emotional and mental discomfort, which in turn can limit your ability to focus on anything productive. This is what to turn to first.

Live your 'VITALS' (Selig, 2016)

Please respond to the following:

VALUES (What traits, behaviours, causes, do you care about?)

INTERESTS (What gives you enjoyment or contributes to your happiness?)

TEMPERAMENT (What are you like . . . really? E.g. low key, impulsive, easy to anger?)

AROUND THE CLOCK (Are you an 'early bird' or a 'night owl'? What is the timeline of your 'perfect day'?)

LIFE MISSION (What are your personal goals? What are the things you have achieved you are proud of?)

STRENGTHS (As YOU see them, and as a CLOSE FRIEND would see them)

Once you recognise what they are, seek ways of making sure your actions are always in tune with them. If you begin to realise that an area of your life is disjointed, that is the area to work on adapting, or being flexible in how you respond to it – including the option of changing or removing it if that is tenable.

Encourage your teams to live their VITALS too – offering support to those who may not be doing so.

Resilience starts from within the self

This chapter has been focused on establishing courage within yourself and the team you currently lead, and therefore these principles will be expanded on from Chapter 3 onwards. The remainder of this book will enable you to do the rest for your current community, and the one which you may choose to grow into. However, it all needs to start with *you*.

If *you* do not value learning and development, how can you inspire others to engage with it? If *you* struggle to appreciate the benefits of change, it is harder for you to embed it in those around you. And if *you* are not strong, you cannot act as a foundation when your teams need support.

Bear this in mind as you (and those you are supporting) progress through the book – especially the notion that, despite all efforts, everyone remains responsible for their own choices – positive or otherwise, and any relapses will hopefully be temporary and obstacles can be overcome.

END-OF-CHAPTER TOOLKIT

ADOPT Resilience now

Act

Start a journal, or use this book as a working document to reflect on your progress. When you notice something unusual in your response, take the time to ask yourself:

1. What did I just do?
2. Why did I respond in that way?
3. Remember, however, you may not find your reasons straight away, but the act of thinking about it is the start of your self-growth.

You may then wish to encourage others to do the same.

Deal

If your initial reflections reveal something which you are able to action or influence, but would simply rather not - dare to address it right now. If you do something, anything, you have opened the possibility of an outcome which may be more positive than a stagnated stalemate.

1. Note the things you have been putting off.

2. Identify which you can influence.

3. Take action (even a small one) on one of those things in (2).

4. Reflect on what you did and the outcome . . . what have you learned from this and would you do something different next time?

Optimise

If you find something works for you, share the good practice with at least one other person; even consider swapping notes on your progress.

1. Identify the people who might benefit from being inspired by your good practice (for example, your children or your team).

2. Begin an open dialogue about your learning process.

Prepare

When attempting or dealing with something which you know may be a stretch for you to complete alone, know who or what your support system is, and the areas in which they contribute the most.

1. Identify your support network (but be specific in how they help you – there is little value in bemoaning something technical to a spouse if solving it is your main aim, as they have no knowledge to do so, but in turn, they may be the most appropriate person for moral support in a different area).

Name:	Area of support:

Thrive

Don't worry if not everyone sees what you are doing straight away. Keep working on different ways to enhance your influence, and be mindful of those who share your passions – they may become even more powerful allies in future.

1. People I connect with:

Notes

> What I did   Date

Reflection (at a later date)

> How have my thoughts changed now?

References

Bounce Back Project https://www.bouncebackproject.org/resilience/ (accessed May 2020).

Defense Logistics Agency https://www.dla.mil/Info/Resiliency/Defined/ (accessed May 2020).

Dr Arielle Schwartz https://drarielleschwartz.com/6-pillars-of-resilience-dr-arielle-schwartz/#.XYIksyhKjIU (accessed May 2020).

EQ Works https://www.eqworks.co.uk/files/8015/2637/8483/6A_-The_Six_Pillars_of_Resilience_v9-2017.pdf (accessed May 2020).

Erikson, E. H. (1958) *Young Man Luther: A study in psychoanalysis and history*. Norton.

Erikson, E. H. (1963) *Youth: Change and challenge*. Basic Books.

People Pleaser Quiz adapted from https://psychologia.co/people-pleaser-quiz/ (accessed May 2020).

Selig, M. (2016) Know yourself? 6 specific ways to know who you are. *Psychology Today* https://www.psychologytoday.com/gb/blog/changepower/201603/know-yourself-6-specific-ways-know-who-you-are (accessed May 2020).

The R@W Sustain Model cited in https://catherinecarr.ca/why-resilience-at-work/ (accessed May 2020).

The Wellbeing Project https://thewellbeingproject.co.uk/5-pillars-of-resilience/5-resilience-pillars22/ (accessed May 2020).

Build strength

2

Reflect

What does strength mean to you?

Many dictionary definitions focus on the idea of physical power, which is somewhat reductionist. Further, any form of learning and development is more effective through knowing *your own* perceptions of the words you use as this makes the outcomes both measurable and meaningful. So consider all questions and reflection points with that in mind. What does it mean to *me* (and then if you are to apply this to your team, what does it mean to *them*)? Perhaps 'strength' is more emotional – it could be the ability to offer support. Maybe it is the ability to beat an enemy. Maybe it is being able to go against the grain with confidence.

When humans were concerned with 'hunter gathering' and the propagation of the species, power and nurture were the archetypical desirable qualities in males and females respectively. The traits of 'strength' were attributed to the male 'Y'-shape physique, i.e. broad shoulders and sturdy legs. Physical strength made a person powerful. However, today many other traits yield power – beauty, talent, intelligence, creativity, innovation, healing, teaching, money (or the capacity to earn it). Power can be derived from a number of sources.

Perhaps the better question as you approach this chapter is: What does strength mean to you in the context of your organisation? (Or what does it mean for you personally if you were looking to develop it in yourself?)

That is, What DOES 'power' look like?

What challenges do you face?

What does success mean in your world?[1]

That will be what you need to build when you think about 'building strength'.

Resilience is likewise targeted. If you know what you need to be strong, you also know what you need to reinforce in case of damage.

Try this

A personal hero-quest

You may not be a Dungeons & Dragons (D&D) player, but for this moment, take this chapter as your game and indulge me.

---

[1] Note that you may also wish to ask yourself these questions in the context of your personal life or relationships as well, in which case your responses may change. People are context dependent, and any form of personal development is best **applied** as relevant to you and your experience, rather than a standard 'Do this and that will happen'.

Character sheet

You can do this for any of the many roles you play – just be clear which one you are thinking about.

Role:		Greatest powers
Unique skills		
Trait	**Competency / 10**	**Weakness (es)**
		Notes

Ask yourself:

▌ How do these traits enable me to be more effective in my role?

▌ What areas can I improve on and why do I want or need to?

As a trainer, I appreciate that co-operative games are, conceptually, an engaging way to learn, and through a metaphorical approach one can reflect and reframe without detriment in daily life. This chapter takes a gaming approach to learning, and now it's time to 'level up'.

Start strong

In the quest mechanic, players 'level up' by gaining 'experience points' – the more they play, the more they learn about the world they are in, the friends and the foes, and the more successful their campaigns. This is in many ways a fantasy world parallel of life. Characters embark on a journey, they form a team, they nurture alliances, overcome barriers, obstacles and enemies, and are often rewarded in gold or accolades. Five simple lessons can be learned from the Dungeon Master (DM), the creator of each story, even before starting out – all are easily applicable to the context of our teams, organisations and other collaborative experiences:

1. Carry the appropriate equipment.

   You wouldn't go on a camping trip without a tent or caravan, why would you take on a project without knowing you have the necessary equipment (or at least where you can access it) to succeed?

   > If you notice technical areas need updating, look into updating them. This applies to knowing what websites your children are using at school – and at home – as much as it does to upgrading a whole system network.

2. Ensure the most useful skills set mix.

   A successful campaign always requires a variety of skills. There is no point having a team of fighters when faced with only supernatural beings, or a team of merchants in a post-apocalyptic scenario. With D&D the balance tends to be: Fighter, Wizard (or spellcaster), Rogue, Ranger and Healer; it is helpful to be aware that you not only have high performers, but a breadth of abilities as well.

> ▌ Be aware of the type of work you and your team will be involved in – not just before each project, but as you look into your future. If the skills set is lacking, it is wise to take steps early to address and improve that.
>
> ▌ Note also that it is not always essential for the team to be friends.
>
> ▌ As well as breadth, it may also be helpful to ensure each member of the team has skills to supplement each other's so that if one person is detained there is someone who is confident and competent in 'placeholding' for them until they return.

3. Remember, there is no fixed script, just a beginning and end.

Some things cannot be predicted nor planned for, but merely dealt with in the aftermath, or responded to on the way. Characters on a campaign often keep the end goal in sight, when dealing with a crisis. For example, why spend valuable time trying to revive a character when they can be carried for the time being? Further, they need to be aware of opportunities that may open up to them as they progress. Yes, they may also bring challenge, but they can also bring rewards, and experience. Players are therefore always actively aware of the skills and items (or 'technology' if referring to a workplace) they possess, and what is going on around them.

> ▌ Always know what you are trying to achieve. This can help make your decision making focused and thus more effective, especially at the point of crisis when thoughts can lack clarity.
>
> ▌ However, bear in mind that although you have an end point, the journey you are taking may take unexpected turns – taking a pro-active and reflective approach to life enables you to foresee potential threats as well as opportunities.

4. Luck can change on the roll of a dice.

You are unable to control the behaviour of others. The only dice you play are your own – and even then a dice role does not necessarily rely on skill. Further, it is as essential to build your own character's survival skills rather than choosing only traits that assist the party – because you never know when your star fighter will roll a 1.

> Focus on setting up your own situation as strongly as possible – even if the dice fall against you, you may yet withstand. Time spent on building yourself up is never wasted.

5. 'Initiative' is sometimes improved by watching and waiting.

'Roll for initiative' is the cry of the DM as characters find themselves within a combat situation. The role decides who goes first and the mini game of fighting the aggressors takes place in that order. There is debate within players who enjoy combat as a definitive part of D&D and those who feel it is jarring to the rest of the story. For these latter players, DMs have been known to give them the opportunity to avoid combat as long as they respond sensitively to the characters that have appeared around them and their environment. Rather than fighting, such encounters have resulted in trading, negotiation and even alliances (The DM Lair, 2020). Even if you are the sort of person who not only runs headlong into battle, but is even *looking* for a fight (perhaps you are energised by winning!?), there can be much enjoyment from a change of pace by taking a different tack – and alliances can even be formed to build towards a greater win in the endgame. After all, the story is as much directed by the player as the creator!

Meet scenarios and reflect on your responses

You will now be given a series of scenarios to consider. There is no right or wrong, but they act as a gateway to your thought process with the aim of encouraging you to think about what you might do, but also look at the reasons for taking that action in case that reveals areas in which you may want to improve.

Scenario 1

You have had a fractious relationship with your line manager for a while, and feel that s/he is taking opportunities to undermine you. Recently s/he has asked if you want to go on an annual event run by the firm. You say you would 'Love to'. A few days later you get an email saying 'Sorry, I had to send the two new starters, and with them included the places were all booked'. You know that one of the new starters didn't want to attend because they had mentioned it to you. What do you do?

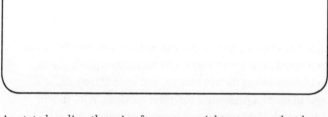

As stated earlier, there is of course no right or wrong, but how many of you were driven to do or say something so you could really 'make the boss feel bad about what s/he did to you'?

This is a common response when one is angry and upset, especially in the light of a history which has been less than harmonious. However, venting your anger is not likely to make any difference – except potentially result in you saying something you may regret; and even the most eloquently worded email about your feelings will not necessarily elicit remorse.

Reflection points

You cannot control how others will respond. No matter how much you want someone to feel something, you cannot force them to do it.

Optical illusions are a common example of how one thing can be perceived in different ways, and sometimes participants have trouble seeing the alternative, and even if they do, still choose to show a preference for 'their version'. With this in mind, something short expressing your disappointment and possibly requesting an action in future may suffice, e.g.

> *'I'm really disappointed to hear that because I said I'd love to have gone. Next time, please let me know if it's only a possibility rather than a definite offer.'*

Of course you may still feel slighted, so:

> Reflect on your history of interactions, and those your line manager has with others – IS it really personal? (Thus, scenario work allows you to think on your response and then reflect on what precipitated it.)

Sometimes we assume that frustrations are aimed personally, when that event may have happened to anyone who was there, or that person behaves in similar ways to others. If, on reflection, you find that it may be personal, then you have a course of action – you may wish to keep a record in order to report it, or perhaps you may wish to leave – either way, you are not sitting and stewing over it, because that will make you feel worse. Research by Steven Parton has found that because each time we think something emotionally similar, the same neuropathways light up; the more we think negatively, the more likely it is for those pathways to fuse (Stillman, 2019). While it is possible to 'retrain' the brain, it certainly seems to suggest that the more you fret over something the more your brain will 'wire itself' negatively. Stillman goes on to add that when you also think that way, being around negativity can be contagious ('Misery likes company'), something which can be trivial can turn into quite a heartache.

If you find you seem constantly disappointed in others, are you asking the wrong questions of them?

... and try this instead

Mindful self-love

Rather than seeking validation from others, which may result in you taking something personally which was not even directed at you, re-energise your brain by doing one tiny thing each day that makes you happy – whether it is a moment

➤

spent looking at a photo of a loved one, or wearing a colour you love, or going for a short walk – even having a drink when you need one. And as you do it, remember you are doing this for you.

Alternatively, and with a calmer frame of mind, accept that people sometimes simply respond in 'their way' and even if you wanted to, you cannot save others from themselves, but you can be less burdened by their behaviours when it comes to managing your future responses.

Consider using your personal power

Ask yourself – could a clearer, or more overt, communication from your side result in a better result? Sometimes people respond in one way because they are unaware that they should respond in a different way. Other times, what we perceive in our heads may not be what has transpired.

. . . for example try this

With a group of people, line them up so they form a queue. Explain you are going to mime a message, and the person you mime it to has to pass it on to the next person and so on. However, state that each person doing the mime has to be very clear what THEY are miming, even if they aren't sure what the person who mimes to them is communicating.

Ask everyone except the person next to you to turn and face the other way.

Mime an action – I use 'getting on a bike, putting in the key, kicking off the brake, revving the engine and driving'. It needs to be a long enough action and the bike example has five components.

> What you will tend to find is that the message is hugely simplified by the end of the line – and there will be a distortion in what people think they are doing. This distortion is often of greatest relevance to them.

Research on memory often reveals the fallibility of the human mind. Bartlett's (1932) War of the Ghosts experiment where he told a story to participants who then recounted it to others, who then did the same and so on, found that participants tended to change details in order to make sense of the story in their heads. Bartlett referred to this as the construction of schemas. Therefore, if you already have a perception in your mind that you respond in a certain way, you are likely to recollect doing so, even if this was not the case. Reflect on your own actions too.

Scenario 2

You know your company is restructuring and this may involve losing some of your team. You have budget left in order to provide training. What do you do?

It may be tempting to offer training on current packages so that the whole team is fully trained and therefore more valuable to the company. You might also consider alternatives such as software or skills that they may require in the future – whether at your company, or within the field – so if any of them do have to move on they are prepared. You might even look at using the budget in order to 'save' your current team.

The most effective initial course of action is to ask them what their current needs are *and* what they may need in the future. Nisbett *et al.* (1973) found that one behaviour could be perceived in different ways depending on whether you were the person doing it (the actor) or the person watching it (the observer). In particular, they noticed that actors tended to attribute negative behaviours to situational factors, while observers attributed those negative behaviours to the actors themselves. While this bias is also relevant when it comes to how your team may perceive your actions in this situation, in the first instance, it is clear that assumptions can often be erroneous, and therefore, opening a dialogue with your team may be beneficial.

Within the scenario, BOTH upskilling for current need and future planning are helpful and ideal if they can be done together. Not only will the team be able to function if people leave it, but your team will feel you have invested in their future. (This is made easier through knowing what your team may wish to do.)

Try this

Can you ask rather than assume?

▌ How do you know your team wants to remain? If you have the liberty of discussing what may happen (and if you do not, ask if you can), it is sometimes more helpful to a team to know what could be happening.

▌ This may also open a good opportunity to look at the areas of strength and weakness in your team in the light of where the company is going.

Another question to ask when building resilience (or indeed strength of any kind, as many fitness professionals would ask), because of the time and effort it takes to achieve results is: 'What are you looking to strengthen?' You need to ask yourself: '. . . what should be resilient; in reaction to what dangers; how should the systems I have respond; and who will benefit?' (Post Carbon Institute, 2017). For the Post Carbon Institute, resilience is not bouncing back but leaping *forward*! Not only is resiliency about '. . . protecting the basic structures of the failed system . . .' but it is also about 'solving problems through innovation . . .' while also being mindful of your surrounding network, especially those that power or invest in the system, and what benefits you wish to achieve.

Therefore, you yourself need to identify what, within you, needs to be strengthened and why, ***bearing in mind where you want to go, why and who with***. This holds true for the skills of your team, and those of your organisation as a whole.

For example . . . try this

Plan ahead

Do you KNOW where your organisation, market and sector will be in 1/3/5 years' time?

Do you know what your clients will want from you in 1/3/5 years' time?

How can you seize an opportunity if you uncover one?

Most leaders will be familiar with the SWOT analysis as conducted on the future direction of the organisation. When using it for the purposes of building resilience, it can be applied personally, i.e. an examination of your personal strengths – or those of your team, or applied to an organisation-wide, or even community-wide approach, or to the needs of your clients.

The basic principles remain the same with the addition of knowing your support network, and a directed focus on what it is you are trying to achieve.

Identify your personal/your organisation's end goal(s)/1, 3, 5 year plan goal(s):

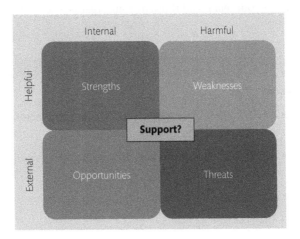

Personal	Organisational
What are my personal strengths?	What are our organisational strengths?
What are my personal areas of weakness (where have I been damaged in the past/where might I be vulnerable right now)?	What are our organisation-wide areas of weakness (where have we been damaged in the past/where might we be vulnerable right now)?
What new opportunities may arise if I pursue these goals? That is, what is my motivation for this end goal or outcome?	What new opportunities may arise if the organisation pursues these goals? That is, what is the motivation for this end goal or outcome?
What threats do I face in pursuing these goals, AND if I should achieve them?	What threats might befall the organisation in pursuing these goals, AND if we achieve them?
(Additional) – Who is within my support network?	(Additional) – Who is within our support network?

The use of the SWOT analysis in this case is less about whether one *should* take action but is more a starting point for the direction in which to build strength when the decision to act has been made. When it comes to resilience, being aware of your strengths and your support network becomes part of managing the threats or weaknesses, and the opportunities form a means of motivation. It is the starting point for growth.

Then, with the weaknesses you have identified, consider them *in the context of the future goal*. There is no point trying to fix everything if things will eventually be redundant.

Know what needs to be strengthened for the most successful or desired outcome bearing in mind the points of current and previous failure, as well as the possible threats you have identified. That becomes your starting point for effort.

Building strength which is targeted is the most effective means of applying (and conserving!) your valuable time and energy.

Use the SWOT analysis to meet future client need too

You can also consider using similar principles with the feedback you get from your clients to learn where they will be, and what you could be doing to provide that service at the very moment they need it.

CLIENT
What are my strengths as the client sees them – why do they come to me?
What are my areas of weakness – where might I be less competitive with other similar organisations?
What new opportunities could I seize upon bearing in mind client future need, timescales and resources?
What threats do I face in pursuing these goals, OR in failing to pursue them?
(Additional) – Who is within my support network whom I can utilise?

If you are going to build – do so in a targeted manner.

Case example: MAHLE Powertrain

Research was conducted into future testing requirements for vehicle emissions. A strong desire was also identified from the client base for a vehicle test facility to include four-wheel drive, climatic and altitude test capabilities. Using this evidence, reprioritising of modest capital expenditure was approved to enable a fast-track and launch of the 'Real Driving Emissions Centre (RDEC)' at the client point of need. This is the first such testing space of its kind in the UK, and the demand for it has exceeded prediction (Sanderson, 2019).

Note, however, in the case of future planning for clients, your opportunities must also always be supported by high-quality research.

Scenario 3

You are in the middle of a tough time at work – your team is running at full pelt. You know that you need to oversee everything, and in doing so you recognise that there are a couple of balls being dropped. How do you respond?

It's often so tempting to jump in, sword raised, but your role as co-ordinator is important. Without someone running the operation, it is not always possible to respond accurately to the full picture. Are the best football captains the star strikers or the goal keepers?

Of course there is a lot more to football captaincy, but this is simply to illustrate the question – are you tactically better in the thick of it, or watching from the back? Both positions are of similar importance!

Reflect on your role:

> *'Once more unto the breach' dear friends, once more'*
>
> (Henry V)

There are many reasons why you run in. You may be the type of person who is always supportive and has built their leadership standing shoulder to shoulder with the team. This can work – actors direct themselves, leaders do jump in to pick up emergencies – but your skills sets are now different, and the team relies on you to co-ordinate as much as to know the job if the situation worsens.

A Fire Chief once explained that he had wanted to support his team so much that he helped with the groundwork at one of his first incidents in his promoted role. Luckily this didn't end up in too much disruption, but the lack of outside co-ordination was felt, and he learned quickly to notice the gaps and deploy accordingly.

Sometimes, you simply need to delegate.

Ensure that your team can be delegated to

Delegation is a skill which not only can empower your team – especially if you keep the lines of communication open with them on what they perceive to be their skills-set needs – but one which also allows you to develop in your role as well. Never forget that you too are moving forward on your journey.

If you want to join in the work effort because you miss it, plan for it and allow for it. But if you are doing it because you don't believe someone else can – that is a problem (so train them). Or if you need a bit of a boost because you are in a new role which may seem daunting and difficult, that too needs to be addressed.

Don't be Peter!

The proverbial 'Peter Principle' is part of a work of satire by William Morrow and Company which states: 'A person is promoted to the level of their incompetence' (Peter and Hull, 1969). It is now used to illustrate the view that some people with perceived severe shortcomings are often promoted.

Sometimes the hired employee is not going to work out, but if your response to the new challenge is by avoiding learning your new job, you may well be culpable.

Try this regularly

Challenge your comfort zone

Remember this from Chapter 1? Building strength is about pushing yourself through the stretch zone and existing in the panic zone until you build your confidence in the area.

Regularly do little things which push you outside your comfort zone, even as simple as ordering a different drink, or upping the ante within a hobby. Even if you have to do these things alone, remember that if you master them, you can then help others who may be afraid.

Building up little acts that broaden your world makes it easier to face - or even take up - a bigger challenge later on.

➤

AND

Should the opportunity arise, be aware of who can support you, but undertake a challenge – you don't even need to tell anyone you are doing it (yet). But perhaps it's something you never thought you would do, or you longed for, or perhaps it is even on your 'bucket list'.

Once you are comfortable again, encourage others through talking about your efforts (and struggles!) as well as celebrating your achievements.

Scenario 4

You are faced with ANY scenario you have been faced with before. What now?

It can be so tempting to simply '. . . do what you've done before' – after all it works – and why shouldn't you?

However, also question why it actually came about? Did you learn anything the last time that could have prevented it?

Don't be like Sisyphus!

The myth of Sisyphus sees the eponymous character push a boulder up the hill, only to see it roll down again every time he came close to the top. You are not doomed to repeat the

> Building inner strength is like building
> physical strength – it just takes practice

same fate, but you must take reasonable steps to learn from the last time.

It is not unreasonable to have the number of a reputable taxi rank to hand on a night out, nor to spend a moment thinking about what led up to an issue so that you can recognise the triggers and take precautions at an earlier point. While this may not always prevent the occurrence, it might just ease the clean-up operation.

Instead try this

Know your 'crisis response'

To borrow a term from Dialectical Behaviour Therapy, in order to support people to manage their emotions, they are often asked to create a 'Crisis Pack' – this includes a means of recognising their emotional triggers; a list of people to call when things get rough; and simple, go-to ways to calm the immediate moment to better 'cope ahead'.

The same can be used for any potential challenge. Think of a scenario that was difficult to resolve and which may occur again:

- What triggered it?
- How did you resolve it?
  - Can anything be put in place to prevent or delay the first point?
  - Can anything be put in place to make the second point quicker?

➤

▌ Who is your support network (who will be suitable in this scenario)?

▌ How can you train yourself/your team to better withstand, or avoid this in future?

Change is not easy – but remember why you started the journey

The Dilts model of change is the most illustrative of the importance of addressing the mind first. Dilts (1998) sets out the process of change as having six levels:

6. **Purpose**: your view of the bigger picture

5. **Identity**: your view of yourself

4. **Beliefs and values**: your reasoning

3. **Capabilities**: your skills

2. **Behaviour**: your actions

1. **Environment**: your surroundings

For Dilts, change can occur at any level of the hierarchy, but if it begins at the lower levels – as is often the easiest – the results will not flow upwards. Make the change at a higher level, and the results permeate down.

As a simple example, many people wishing to lose weight may join a gym (change of environment). They may even go a few times (a change in behaviour), they may get stronger (increased capability), but unless they begin to enjoy exercise, or find a way of connecting mentally with either the results or the action they are taking, many will stop and old habits resume. The most successful change occurs when you can establish the reasons WHY someone may choose to be more healthy (the purpose, or their identity or their belief) and when you can tap into that, the rest follows more swiftly.

Reflect

What's your WHY?

Being self-aware of your authentic desires (even if they may not be palatable to others, e.g. a wish to lose weight to look good in a bikini rather than for 'good health' may seem superficial to some) helps you not only to maintain, but also to keep making improvements in that area, especially when things get tough. You are building resilience within yourself after all. How much does it really matter if your choices (as long as they are not directly hurtful to others) are interpreted?

Write yours now:

Always keep that in mind, and with the exercises in this chapter under your belt, you're ready to level up!

END-OF-CHAPTER TOOLKIT

ADOPT Resilience now

Act

Reflect on the importance of being multi-faceted. It is not always possible to have all the skills you need yourself, at least not to the degree of 'expert'. (Even D&D characters have

their own special skills, and rely on each other for support.)
Success today also calls for a variety of abilities and while
flexibility is advantageous, you do not need to be all things
to all people. Be honest in your self-reflections and develop
what you can, or what is most essential for peak performance
in your role, and ensure you know who in your network
covers the remaining bases.

Deal

When it comes to dealing with issues, frustrations and
setbacks are common, so try to have simple, easy-to-access
things to be able to calm your mind in order to return to
the task at hand refreshed. While you might say that you
enjoy spa days or holidays, both take planning and other
resources, have something easy to reach so that relaxation
is more immediate (Hicks, 2019). Think about whether you
need a distraction such as a puzzle app or book; or whether
something tactile might ground you. I carry a fan so I can
immediately change the temperature when I am 'worked up'
about something. Use the following instruction **IF** X happens
THEN I will . . .

Optimise

If you find something that works – share it. Make reflection
and personal development a part of your team meetings or
briefings, so that everyone is able to benefit from healthy
practices.

Prepare

Don't wait until a crisis – use the examples in this chapter and
other simple scenario thought experiments to identify any
weaknesses and work to reinforce them now. As any fitness
professional will tell you, physical strength training can be
targeted, and this can be applied to mental strength too. Try
not to just focus on what is easy – challenge yourself.

> **Thrive**
>
> Find time to celebrate what you have. The path of self-development is an ongoing one, and where you have come from is as important as where you are going for who you are right now. *Ask yourself – 'In this situation, what would I have said or done a year ago?', and reflect on how things have changed within you.*

Notes

What I did	Date

Reflection (at a later date)

> How have my thoughts changed now?

References

Bartlett, F. C. (1932) *Remembering: A study in experimental and social psychology.* Cambridge University Press.

Dilts, R. (1998) *Modeling with NLP.* Meta Publications.

Dilts model of change cited by NLP podcast (2020) https://nlppod.com/nlp-logical-levels/(accessed May 2020).

Hicks, R. (2019) Dr Rob Hicks on Wellbeing at the Canela Café, *The Chrissy B Show, Sky 191* https://youtu.be/5eP0pnywJ7c (accessed November 2020).

Nisbett, R. E., Caputo, C., Legant, P. and Marecek, J. (1973) Behavior as seen by the actor and as seen by the observer.

Journal of Personality and Social Psychology, Vol. 27, No. 2, 154–164.

Peter, L. J. and Hull, R. (1969) *The Peter Principle*. William Morrow & Co Inc (Pan Books edition 1970).

Post Carbon Institute (2017) Resilience program https://www.postcarbon.org/program/resilience/ (accessed May 2020).

Sanderson, D. (2019) Talk on MAHLE Powertrain capabilities, May 2020 https://www.mahle-powertrain.com/en/capabilities/rde-development-testing/ (accessed September 2020).

Stillman, J. (2019) Need some good news? The 5 happiest headlines of 2019 so far, *Inc.* https://www.inc.com/jessica-stillman/the-5-happiest-headlines-of-2019-so-far.html (accessed May 2020).

The DM Lair (2020) https://www.youtube.com/watch?v=TNoaIHWFHIs (accessed January 2020).

Attract, maintain and retain courageous teams

> Repeat after me:
>
> *I cannot control the outcome*
>
> *The bravest thing I can do is show up.*

I treat affirmations in the way that psychologist Richard Wiseman does – if you tend to notice what you think about, isn't it better that what you think about is positive? His example is to **NOT** think of a pink elephant. When that thought is introduced, it's really not easy to avoid thinking it. It's also the reason why when you think about buying something specific, you suddenly seem to see more people with it; or you get that feeling of 'Oh where was that when I needed it' as the shops suddenly seem stocked with whatever it was you were searching for. It may not be that anything has changed, but simply that you have primed your mind to notice.

Therefore, if you want to bring those courageous people who live your values into your organisation (or life) – you need to start living them yourself.

Recruit for value

> *If you have not yet completed the VITALS exercise from Chapter 1 please do so now.*

The counter position to those who share your outlook being drawn to you is that those who do not may become more distant – or you may feel them fading from your life. While this is not always comfortable, there is never anything wrong with curating your relationships. When your values are not shared by those closest to you, conflict is more likely to ensue than collaboration. While conflict is often the catalyst for innovation, it can as easily become a fight to *win* rather than get anything done . . . especially when values – the fundamental beliefs you hold – are part of the problem.

Try this

Write down what you believe your personal or organisational values to be:

Now reflect on your current actions (personally if that is your focus or) as your organisation. What might others believe them to be?

As an example, during a training session in one institution I noted that while the values stated 'Excellence' and 'Inclusivity', what those who worked there actually felt the values were included 'Hitting targets' and 'Money'. I observed further that those who were the happiest within that organisation were those who were driven by the latter two – i.e. the values that were being *lived* – and there was unhappiness and cynicism within the rest of the team. It is notable that the staff members who found their situation 'tenable' were those whose personal skills enabled them to hit targets because they felt 'Outside the line of fire' – but they also did not report strong feelings of happiness with the ethos the organisation was living (despite what it said it valued).

> So now think about those you are surrounded by. If you find a disconnect between your personal/your organisation's values and what you see is being lived, reflect on whether you are happy with the personalities you most often see.

> *'You can tell the measure of a man by the company he keeps.'*
>
> (Spanish proverb)

Despite what you may profess to believe in, if you do not actively *live* it you may find yourself surrounded with people who connect with the behaviour you are *projecting*, rather than what you might want to believe in.

If you want to change that – start changing your actions.

Live your values.

Maybe the time is not right

There may be good reasons as to why action should be staid, but at some point it must be taken.

Resilience is about having the courage to face the darkness, and sometimes doing so without much of a safety net.

> Even the best conceived planning and
> analysis is no substitute for taking action

From an organisational point of view, this may mean even a restructure at the very core, but once the dust has settled you are left with a wonderful opportunity to rebuild.

Ask yourself

What is the worst thing that can happen if you assert your values?

Then decide, if you cannot live with that, what are your options?

By being aware of the bottom line, you may be able to find an acceptable balance.

Then take action – even if you cannot predict the outcome.

All too often what tends to happen is your desire to know that 'it'll all be ok' holds us back . . . the truth is *you cannot predict an outcome when dealing with people – there are too many variables.* You can certainly set things up the best you can to go a certain way (you can 'prepare'), but there are 'loose cannons', there are things going on in people's lives which we have no idea about that can affect their behaviours, and the only actions you have control over are *yours.*

The problem of 'atychiphobia'

The fear of failure (or literally 'fear of the unfortunate') is not only paralysing but exhausting in its paralysis. The lack of action taken often leads to further anxiety and can continue the spiral down into depression. *The Active Times*

(Dossantos, 2016) reports that while you may prefer to be alone when anxious, this allows anxiety to retain its hold over you. Anxiety is very real, and while I would not necessarily advocate the old adage of 'feel the fear and do it anyway there and then', you are certainly still better off finding an active method of working through your feelings.

While self-reflection is a positive thing to do, it can sometimes – especially for the more cerebrally driven – become a 'safe retreat' of avoidance. If you get to the point where you are reflecting more and more to '. . . just get that answer . . .' your behaviour may have gone beyond what is helpful to you.

Simply, there is no point investing in learning if you do not utilise the returns – OR if you try to use them all at once. If you *practise* what you have discovered, you will also begin to work out what is most effective in which situation. The truth is, you really must, at some point, 'feel the fear and do it anyway' (Jeffers, 2007).

Recruit for proficiency

Try this

List the proficiencies that you have.

Now think about the contexts in which they have been the most useful:

Proficiency	Contexts in which I have used/could use this skill
E.g. Awareness of others' feelings	Changing tack in a pitch; mentoring; team meetings; knowing when to leave an argument or when to ask a favour; reading the room in a presentation
Discipline	Getting projects to the end point; keeping a large team focused

Proficiency	Contexts in which I have used/could use this skill

To take this a step further, think about the same proficiencies and consider when you have used them ineffectively:

Proficiency	Contexts in which I have used this skill ineffectively
E.g. Awareness of others' feelings	To suppress my own feelings in order to fit in with a crowd I didn't want to fit in with
Discipline	Beating myself up or feeling consumed by guilt over not sticking to my diet

All the energy you have spent on the inefficient tasks will likely have prevented you from focusing fully on the efficient ones. Your energy, like your time, is a finite quality – so spend it wisely.

An inventory of skills

To avoid the problem of overthinking it is helpful to see learning new skills not as extra weight, but as part of a growing inventory. You never need to use them all at once, neither do you necessarily need to forget or dismiss the older behaviours you used to prefer. See them as an inventory and actively select which will be of most use in any given situation.

By that token, organisation-wise, a skills audit on your team can be helpful too and if you don't have some skills, that's when you may need to add staff members, contractors or collaborators – while remembering that values matter too.

To perform a skills audit, you can use a table similar to the one presented below:

	People in team with listed skills			
Skills required				

Such an audit may also be a good starting point for discussion – you could use it to ask team members if there are areas they would like to develop prior to bringing in more recruits.

Recruit for courage

Note, however, in the same way as it is possible to hold one set of values in your mind, and present quite another through your actions as discussed at the start of this chapter, others can too. It is easily possible to 'talk the talk' within an interview setting with evidence and rehearsed examples of leadership and problem solving, but in situ it's quite a different matter.

This is where the 'assessment day' style of recruitment is one of the most effective methods, and it doesn't even need to take a long time, if you know how to optimise it.

Try this

1. How would you rate yourself on a scale of 1-10 on perseverance, problem solving and open mindedness?

2. Now work out the following:

> **Puzzle 1:**
>
> Last in the first
>
> Last in the second
>
> Forget the third
>
> First in the fourth
>
> Last in the fifth
>
> Know what is best for you and be wise
>
> Life will often give you many choices
>
> Think twice before following the crowd blindly
>
> Bring yourself the best opportunities
>
> Aim high, even if you have to work a little harder with offering rewards
>
> **Puzzle 2: (clue: the alphabet gets in the way)**
>
> ARBECCDREUFIGTHWIIJSKELLMYN

The answers are in the footnote.[2]

---

[2]Puzzle 1 - the hint is in the first 'poem' - it's the last word in the first sentence, the last word in the second and so on. The answer reads: 'Wise choices bring rewards.'
Puzzle 2 - remove the alphabet which is in between the words. The answer reads 'Recruit wisely'.

These are two simple examples of my 'escape room' style puzzles which I use to look at team relationships, and have used as part of a recruitment process. The 'live escape room' concept began in 2012 in Hungary, and based itself on the Japanese computer games where teams were locked in a room and had to solve puzzles in order to 'escape'. It's similar in concept to The Crystal Maze (which itself has a 'live version' in London and Manchester). Each game is timed to 1 hour. While it is possible to hire such venues and watch interviewees via the CCTV by arrangement with the facility, I use a 'tabletop'[3] version that up to 80 can play at any one time. What is revealed over the duration is a more in-depth presentation of what you might have felt tackling the above puzzles, i.e.

Reflect

▌ Did you give up and skip to the footnote?

▌ Did you think 'this is ridiculous'?

▌ Did you consider 'this is great, I wonder if there are more'?

▌ Did you just ignore it?

▌ Anything else???

And now think about:

What were your rankings on the questions at the start?

▌ perseverance

▌ problem solving

▌ open mindedness

(that is, if you even answered them!!)

▌ Would you say you were someone who persevered . . . if so why did you skip to the footnote?

▌ Would you say you were open minded . . . if so why might you think 'this is ridiculous'?

. . . and so on.

---

[3] https://youtu.be/DE1aNcC6ht0

Within the enjoyment and time pressure of the escape game (many are hugely immersive, the award-winning 'Panic Room'[4] in Gravesend Kent has one of the largest selections including horror, 'Jurassic Park' and even a 'Wizard of Oz' themed room) people forget their inhibitions, and often what they've said of themselves on their CVs. They may get frustrated, they may try to dominate, they may withdraw. While this is not necessarily exactly indicative of their behaviour within a business-specific situation, the escape room draws upon the most valuable skills – the transferrable ones: determination, motivation, teamwork, leadership, communication, listening, logic, creativity, organisation and the like. Resilience is looking at the foundation – recruit the truth, not the image. The image may not sit in strong foundations.

It's very possible to 'fake' an interview, and if you aren't careful, you might think you're getting Dr Quinzel, but end up with Harley Quinn.

Retaining courage

Rose and Dade (2007) discussed the 'Values Modes' scale, which sought to explain the voting strategies of the UK public. Conceptually, people could be divided into taking a pioneering (innovative, developmental) approach to their society, a settler (home maker, quiet comfortable life) perspective or a prospector (opportunistic) viewpoint. While this was originally used to analyse and capitalise on voter mentality which could affect campaign strategy in elections, this model can also be applied to organisations (which can be small societies within themselves).

Once you have recruited your teams, it is helpful to know what – as additional to sharing your values – has brought them to your door. For example, do they want a chance to

---

[4] www.thepanicroom.net

grow, sharpen and apply their skills (pioneers) through the backing of the company? Are they there because they like what they see and know they can be happy performing a job they love? Or do they love your organisation's success and feel they can be part of its ascendance?

Pioneers will tend to be motivated by growth and development; settlers by a sense of consistency and security; prospectors by accolade and recognition. This doesn't mean that you cannot motivate the person driven by growth with praise or any combination of positive opportunity or reassurance, but a reminder that you need a broad approach to continuing to nurture your teams' individual needs.

Try this

Identify what you currently do in order to:

Develop teams	Recognise teams	Ensure a sense of security

Reflect on how you currently offer the above opportunities. For example, is training a 'you will all learn . . .' or more of a 'we have this selection on offer . . .'?; are people's financial claims paid on time and you aren't going into the third restructure in as many years?; do you know what each team member is individually shining in so as to target your praise rather than a group acknowledgement?

Identify ways of bridging any gaps.

Break down silos through a learning and development ecosystem

When it comes to providing opportunities for your teams to grow, remember that there are many approaches beyond the conventional forms of training. Access to field-specific forums; to talks, networks and conferences; or even regularly learning from each other can bring rewards in terms of building relationships, recognition and the confidence to approach others.

Working in silos may not be demanded, but it can sometimes become the 'norm'. Many organisations have found at least one or two people willing to reach back when they've made the first attempt to reach out, and sometimes realising that you are in collaboration rather than competition is a lesson that will keep on giving.

Try this

Turn to the detachable sheets at the end of this chapter. In a team meeting divide your team into groups and simply give each group one or two of the code sheets (in any order) and a copy of the decoder. Say NOTHING else other than – here's your task.

The answers are in the footnote.[5]

This is another of my training exercises derived from my 'Tabletop Escape'/Escape Room puzzles. What I notice when I deliver this is that not only do groups stick together at first, but they become very secretive when they realise they have worked out the code.

---

[5]Decode using the shapes, e.g. if you look at the decoder, 'A' is a backward L, 'B' is a U shape, 'C' is a forward L; the coloured block in the top left denotes the place in the sentence the decoded word goes, hence why you can distribute the codesheets out of order; and the sentence translates as TEAMS ALWAYS THRIVE ON EMPOWERMENT OVER EXPECTATION.

> Gradually they begin to realise – especially when they start thinking about whether they really HAVE 'finished' – that they need to work with other groups to understand the sentence, and once they do that they also begin to interact and help each other by supporting those who hadn't worked out the code through teaching and explanation.
>
> Reflecting on this process gives you a very easy way to open the dialogue on collaborative growth.

'Life is all about facing your fears.' The Wonderful Wizard of Oz.'

(Baum, 1900)

Courage cannot be gained nor lost, it just needs to be exercised.

Courageous acts may bring courageous people; courageous changes may retain them; but courage, while it can be en*courage*d simply needs *continuous practice*.

The more you do something, the more adept you become at it. Researchers in sport science have found that the more an athlete practises a skill, the more mastery they attain and the more confidence they report in repeating that particular action and believing it will go well (National Research Council, 1994). This is true of anything you may have had to learn: the more rehearsal, the better the performance (*despite feeling nervous*).

Courage is about trying it – especially if you believe *it* will bring you the rewards you seek. It is about picking yourself up and learning from what went wrong, or what could go better when doing it again. It is not about confidence. Confidence is knowing that you will be able to 'wing it'. It comes usually when you are just pushing the 'stretch zone' in an area that you're already experienced in (it's the bit that allows you to think – if all else fails, I'll just revert to what

I know). Courage has no safety net. It's about daring to be vulnerable because there is no easy exit. But the rewards are great – and the journey exhilarating.

Be brave. Then don't worry about controlling the outcome . . . you're resilient, you'll cope. And show up.

END-OF-CHAPTER TOOLKIT

ADOPT Resilience now

Act

Identify and try to always live your values, and you will draw those who also connect with them to you. This world is one which can often be unkind, but this does not mean you cannot create at least a small oasis of your own to retreat to. Identify the three values you subscribe to most of all, and try to do something every day that allows you to be proud of yourself for living them – not just knowing them.

Deal

Keep strong. Focus that effort you might have spent helping someone who might not return the 'favour' on something which energises you. (. . . and find a way of offering them support through empowerment instead; for example, asking them what THEY think they could do, or giving them a template to ground their ideas in). That way, when they are ready to come back, you are similarly revived. Go for that run, have that cup of coffee in a favourite spot, read that book – after all the strongest you is the most powerful you.

Optimise

If you are going to do it, make it count. When I was a drama teacher, I taught drama, but I also taught presentation skills, confidence, teamwork and discipline; some students learned that – others just learned drama. If you are going to do it, don't just do it well, but get as much out of it as you can. Experiences don't have to be formal to hold a life lesson or a skill.

Whether it is a professional or personal goal, aim high – know your effort will be worth the eventual reward, and never lose yourself to get there! When doubts creep in, simply ask 'what story am I telling myself and why?'. Often your reasons may be related beyond the situation at hand, and they are only present because of your fear to take the current step.

Prepare

Get into the mindset to embed the world you want by living it. Say to yourself 'I know I am doing a good job'. Never underestimate a tiny act of kindness – a simple 'well done' for your 'prospectors', a request for input – then appreciation of the suggestion even if you don't/can't use it for your 'pioneers', a reminder that you are on the side of your team for the 'settlers' . . . and this also means offering ways to develop people, improve them and have tougher conversations as gently as possible if they need to be had.

Thrive

Show up, be there. We don't have phones just to talk about ourselves on social media, the best connections – at least to my mind – still go on in real life! If someone you love hasn't called you for a while and you want to hear from them, call them, drop them a text – simply let them know you have their back! For your teams, try to recognise their individual value, and even ask them where they would like your support – it doesn't need to take long, you can simply tell them to think about it and let you know . . . then really work at doing something to progress their development – and their trust in telling you.

Notes

What I did   Date

Reflection (at a later date)

How have my thoughts changed now?

References

Baum, F. L. (1900) *The Wonderful Wizard of Oz*. George M Hill Company.

Dossantos, N. (2016) 6 things that make anxiety worse. *The Active Times* https://www.theactivetimes.com/fitness/your-first-time/6-things-make-anxiety-worse (accessed May 2020).

Jeffers, S. (2007) *Feel the Fear and Do It Anyway*. Vermilion.

National Research Council (1994) *Learning, Remembering, Believing: Enhancing human performance* https://www.nap.edu/read/2303/chapter/13#174 (accessed May 2020).

Rose, C. and Dade, P. (2007) Using Values Modes. *Campaign Strategy* http://www.campaignstrategy.org/articles/usingvaluemodes.pdf (accessed May 2020).

Wiseman, R. (2004) *The Luck Factor*. Arrow.

DECODER

CODE SHEETS (to give out in any order)

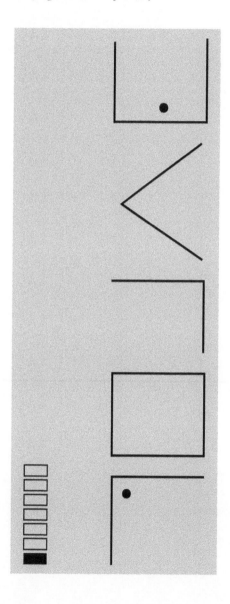

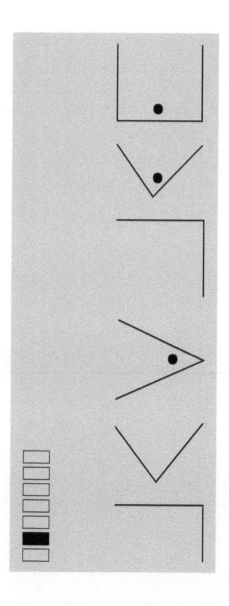

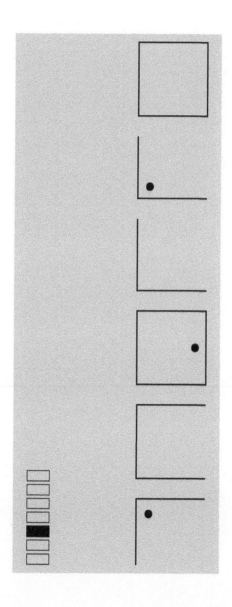

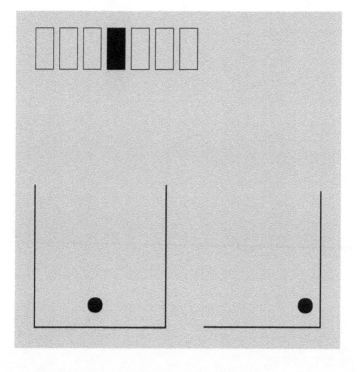

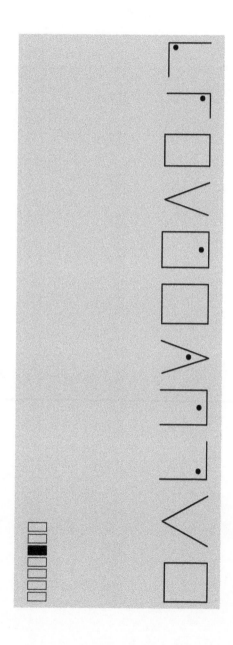

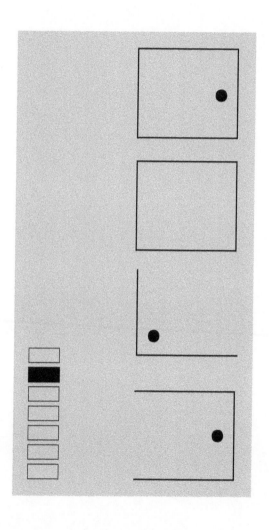

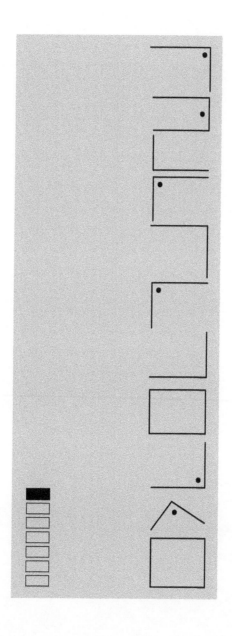

Harness drive and inspire passion

Despite organisations having a shared goal, no one owes you their time or energy – they have their own lives and priorities, as do you. While the extrinsic motivators of money (and related job security) may be drivers to keep people within a team, if you can harness their drive and passion to contribute to the best of their talents while they are there (and then keep them), they play a huge role in organisational resilience, longevity and success.

Why don't they care? (You always seem more passionate than your teams)

The problem for the passionate and driven leader is that they sometimes end up with an enthusiastic team of disciples driven by good results rather than empowered leaders driven by their passion. Of course, the brilliant and passionate leader knows that the added ingredient of love often is what brings the best results – but getting your team to see that is another matter.

It is probably wise to take a moment right now to realise that it's probably not that they don't care – they wouldn't be in the job if they didn't have drive – but that their endgame may be a little different from yours.

As a leader you have had years of experience doing what you enjoy and reaping the rewards, often your teams need to be confident they are earning rewards first. It's important you first look from their perspective of growing rather than from your own of helping them grow . . . and *then letting them*!

Ask your teams

▌ What are their hopes for their future role (within or outside your organisation)?

▌ How would they like you to help them develop?

These two questions also have the benefit of getting your teams to think about their future in a way that the pressures of their job may not allow them to do as readily.

You've no need to be Lady Macbeth

'Hie thee hither, That I may pour my spirits in thine ear;'

(Lady Macbeth, William Shakespeare, Act 1, sc 5)

Reflect

Do you want your teams to be passionate so badly that you can't help giving them a nudge?

If you are a passionate and driven person, and enjoy being around those who feel the same, when you are experienced in a specific field (as you will be in a workplace leadership role), although you want to give your teams ownership, you may be pushing them towards doing it your way (a way that works or a way you love) rather than letting them discover it for themselves. While Lady Macbeth's actions were less virtuous, the sense of overarching control imposed may well be the same.

When in a leadership position, because of the very nature of that position, coupled with your experience (and even more probable if your team likes and/or respects you), if you are asking to see work, they will likely defer to you as a matter of course.

Have you ever

- Questioned why people who are so talented don't seem to have the same drive as you?
- Been frustrated because your teams aren't grabbing what is clearly an opportunity within their reach?
- Wondered why, although your team are really capable, they seem to hold back?

The first question to ask yourself is '*Are you micro-managing?*'

If you have tasked someone with a job, do you let them do it and only advise when they seek it, or do you keep an eye out and nudge when *you* think it's needed?

While this nudge (often) comes from a place of support, it can have the opposite effect.

> '*Yes I was doing it! I just put it down to come here to be reminded to do what I'm already doing, I mean what's the point, why are you calling me to see if I'm doing it, what's the bloody point, I'm doing it aren't I?*'
>
> (Basil Fawlty, Cleese and Booth, 1998)

At best it can sound like a nag, which, after an outburst of frustration, still results in the task being done; but at worst it can affect the self-confidence of the person undertaking the task – and this effect is made worse when you are perceived as more expert than them, *and* they like you!

Quick tips

If you are worried about micromanaging, try the following:

- Ask yourself why you are micromanaging. (Is it because you don't trust your team? Or because they are untrained? Or because there's no time to wait for them to learn?) Once you identify the underlying issue, deal with THAT and the micromanaging will cease.

- Reflect on how you would feel if you were micromanaged and how it might affect your performance.

- Question whether you made the task delegated clear enough so that your team:

  - Knows exactly what the task is

  - Knows the delivery date

  - Knows when and how they can ask for help

  - Knows what is expected of them.

- If you cannot help but put your own input in – even when a task is performed well – ask yourself why you aren't choosing to focus that extra energy and insight into developing your own role or work further.

'You have more power if people like you.'

(James Hunt to Niki Lauda, *Rush*, Morgan, 2011)

Remember, even when your teams are passionate about something, they may defer to you.

Often the person to be promoted is the '. . . charismatic leader [who] motivates people [rather than] . . . the sharply intelligent person who rubs folks the wrong way now and then in pursuit of the truth' writes Mary Faulkner (2018) in her blog '*Surviving Leadership*'. She goes on to note that when leaders are liked, their mistakes might be given 'more grace', they may have 'higher close rates' and it is easier to 'influence and lead'. However, she notes, charismatic James Hunt only won one championship, Niki Lauda won three.

The likability of a leader, especially if they often try to help can, ironically, be disempowering to their teams. If you are nudged by someone you like, you're more likely to go along. This is true professionally as well – after all we are still the same people, just in different clothing.

Reflect

If you are doing the nudging, then the second question to ask yourself is *why?*

- Are you afraid of being left out?
- Do you REALLY think they cannot do it?
- Do you simply care too much?

In the first instance, the self-reflection work in this book or individual coaching may help you address that, and in the second, perhaps direct training – although perhaps more time consuming – is a more effective solution.

Or the possible third option – that you care so much about your teams that you want to ensure they have every chance of success and therefore help where you can.

In this third instance, this is on the one hand hugely positive and supportive. On the other it can be clipping their wings without anyone really realising. As their leader, teams will automatically seek validation from you, and in order for them to grow, you have to have a point in a project at which you stop offering it (e.g. the theatre director never directs from the wings when the actors take the stage to perform, although they may be there to help out if things go wrong and the actors cannot solve it themselves); or you need to be strict with the amount of input you offer . . . even if you think an outcome could be enhanced. If you do not, you will always be factored into everything they do (because they know you

can, could and would help – and often improve their work),
but they will not be flying completely solo.

Provide means, motive and opportunity to succeed

If you wish people were as committed or as passionate as
you to your cause, remember this: people aren't deliberately
choosing *not* to follow their passion. To be doing a job you
love, in a company that you enjoy being part of is a rare
and valuable thing. To have their job, they often have the
means/ability; if they like the company they often have the
motivation – *what they might lack is the opportunity.*

> Teams often have means and
> motivation, leaders who provide the
> opportunity will nurture and retain them

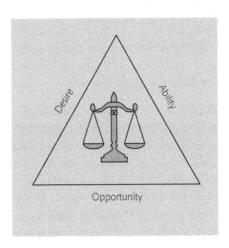

The 'crime triangle' (Eck, 2010) suggests that the instigation
of a criminal event requires all three elements – so too does

progression to success. The 'crime triangle' premise is that for most crimes to occur all three elements need to be fulfilled. Remove one, and it can be prevented. Add whichever element is missing rather than simply pushing what is already there and you get your result. This can also work when nurturing passion within your team.

Ask yourself

▌ How easy is it for your team to focus on the enjoyment of the project rather than results?

▌ Is there a need for targets (sales, financial, satisfied customers) to be made – if not by you, by the organisational culture?

▌ Is progression or appraisal focused on project completion alone?

▌ Do you, or other potential mentors, have time to train or offer support, which takes time, rather than offer immediate solutions?

Most staff members bring their own desire (motivation) and ability, but often the focus within the organisation rests on praise (desire/motivation) or correction/training (ability). Instead give them the chance, or the opportunity, to shine. Consider if you can *trust* them rather than teach them.

Try this

How would you be able to give your teams the opportunity to indulge in their passion (without focusing on targets, reward, or outcome . . . simply enjoying the ability to do it)?

Finding time for passion within work targets

Even if not formal, passion can be fanned informally.

Ask yourself

What social problem do I care about?

How can your organisation make a contribution to solving that problem (however small, within the working procedures)? If you care about mental health, can you encourage people to share what makes them happy, and to have a reminder of that on their desks? If you care about sustainability, can you get your team to avoid single-use plastics? Can you make it a collaborative task, or even a challenge?

Now try this

At an upcoming briefing or meeting, find out what your teams are passionate about.

Then ask yourself how you can innovate something so that they can be supported in their drive. Could you have a competition? An event? Classes?

How can you communicate to the rest of the organisation – and perhaps the outside world – that you are starting a social revolution? (And if you cannot do it – who can ...? Remember, it's that balance of skills again: while beyond the community notice board, you may have familiarised yourself with newsletters, emails and blogging – is there a better reach out there ... and who can best attain it for you?)

Every person you work with, everything you do – that's an opportunity to make a difference – if not on a wider scale, at the very least within your immediate environment.

You are creating the OPPORTUNITY for people to care – firstly without effect on outcome, but perhaps then they are able to see how often the 'special ingredient' in most successes is indeed love!

> Next ask them to revisit the question and create their own opportunities!

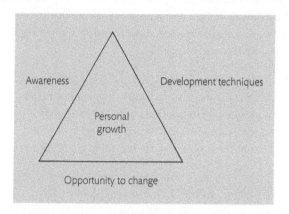

These are the three components needed to harness drive and inspire passion (improving expression of innovation within teams) and it is unlikely to occur when any are missing:

1. Awareness – One needs to be aware that their current or habitual practice is ineffective. This conclusion may be reached by 'going round in circles' or an astute observation within coaching, training or appraisal. It may also come through a careless remark, or perhaps a conflict, or an observed gradual disengagement of teams.

2. Development techniques – One must be given the tools to make a change, should they wish. You cannot shout at someone for 'doing it wrong' and expect them to learn the

'correct method' without showing them. The wise coach, or leader, assumes that people do not deliberately choose to 'misbehave' but rather that they may not know what is expected . . . the first chance – the offering of learning is essential.

3. Opportunity to change, try out, grow – This includes time and a safe space. One will struggle breaking the 'habits of a lifetime', and slip ups may occur. Support to continue on a positive route is essential.

Behaviours that make the person growing feel ashamed, awkward or defensive are of no help – you cannot make fun of someone and then ask them why they stopped doing what they had started. Nor can you say you want ideas and shout them down or 'tweak' them to fit with your vision.

As it is with crime, so is it with teams taking initiative – it is opportunity that is often the most difficult to provide as it requires the greatest amount of work – and patience. Yet, also as with crime, it is the one we have the most control over.

Note also that a lack of opportunity can diminish desire. Taking the subject of crime, remove the opportunity and the 'victim' is less desirable, the same can be said for the motivation of your staff members. Remove opportunity and motivation is adversely affected. If your teams are sent on future-forward courses (ability) with no opportunity to practice their skills, not only will they begin to feel the course was a waste of time (which can then extend to 'training' in general), but unpractised, the skills will wane so should the need arise, they may be rusty. Further, if someone is extremely motivated (desire) when they join a company and find no opportunity to develop, their desire wanes, and they may seek new opportunity elsewhere.

Remember, most people have the means and motive, how can you create the opportunity?

Changemaking – instilling the opportunity to express passion on a broader scale

Ashoka U's Changemaker manifesto[6] is a global strategic plan to cultivate students as changemakers in order to best prepare future leaders to tackle the future's problems. Since 2008 there are now over 500 Changemaker campuses globally which are not only in themselves innovative by design,[7] but part of the academic education includes inviting students to recognise social problems and solve them – using what they are learning from their discipline.

One such example comes from the University of Northampton where a student researching COPD (chronic obstructive pulmonary disease) began a choir for sufferers which, through increasing their sense of camaraderie and bringing unity and fun into their exercise, not only saw huge progress in all participants, but also replicated his work around the country (Mark Blaber, Changemaker Team, University of Northampton). The students had the means, he had the motivation, the Changemaker Hub gave him the opportunity.

---

[6] https://ashokau.org/
[7] The University of Northampton, Waterside is one of the group and as well as responding to student needs such as removing lecture halls at the request of students for a more 'seminar-style' education, they have regenerated a derelict site into an award-winning campus, even boasting its own biomass energy centre and district heating scheme as part of its commitment to sustainability.

While it is not always easy to find the funding, if the drive is there, and no-one says you 'can't' . . . why not step away from the standard operating procedure?

Of course, such opportunities are not to detract from your contracted work, but are about allowing your passion and drive to bloom.

Provide a healthy learning environment

Think back to when you were a baby learning to walk. The environment was full of support and time. You weren't rushed, you weren't trying to master a skill to meet a deadline, and it didn't matter if you fell down. That is the most appropriate environment for training. Is this present for your team?

Ask yourself

▌ What sort of training do you offer?

If most of it is 'hard-skills' based, then while you will certainly have a well-equipped and able team, this will do little for igniting the flame of passion.

▌ If you do offer soft-skills training, how do you offer it?

▌ Can teams take time out to train or are they spending training sessions looking at work back at the office?

▌ Also – consider the ability to practise the training. Often, when you take a moment to reflect on training, how much of it, as inspirational as it might have been, was a series of models and theories which, if you were lucky, you might have had the chance to practise? Training (or even one-to-one meetings or team briefings) affords you time – how can you best optimise it to create *an environment with an emphasis on learning rather than teaching?*

Thought experiment:

You are going to teach your team how to become good leaders – like you. How?

You might have:

▌ identified the qualities of good leaders and perhaps turned that into an activity where teams list the qualities they admire;

▌ asked them to clarify what tasks a leader must undertake;

▌ given them leadership scenarios to solve;

▌ got them to analyse the leadership mistakes in a case study and why they were made;

▌ required them to evaluate the difference between different approaches to leading;

▌ allowed them to create their own manifesto for leading their own teams.

Perhaps you may also have noted the use of Bloom's Taxonomy in the above teaching outline? It is one of the structures trainers are encouraged to use in order to achieve learning outcomes through different levels of thinking.

Bloom's Taxonomy (1956) includes six stages of teaching, each eliciting a greater depth of learning.

▌ Identify: start with a basic understanding of a topic by asking '**identify**' type questions;

▌ Explain: progress to '**explanation**' (in the above example I used 'clarify') in order to appreciate what learners understand;

▌ Apply: **apply** their information – which may sometimes be enough for some learners;

▌ Understand theoretically: take them further and use analysis to show that they **understand** the area in a theoretical or wider approach;

▌ Evaluate: **evaluate** it;

▌ Enhance/Create: and finally take ownership of what they have learned by using it to **create** their own approach to the topic.

If you have proposed something like the above, this would certainly be a very satisfactory lesson. Your delegates will have had a chance to reflect, even practise, and perhaps even be motivated to progress into leadership themselves.

They will then leave the session and feel well trained for leadership, but not necessarily have the passion for why it's important to do it well.

But is that enough?

How can you get them to *think* like leaders, rather than learn the principles alone. Growth is about assimilating knowledge, not just learning it.

Consider the SWOT analysis and GROW coaching models to nurture a leadership *mindset*

Most of you will be familiar with the use of the SWOT analysis – we used it previously in Chapter 2.

1. Set a leadership goal and ask them to conduct a SWOT analysis:

SWOT ANALYSIS

Opportunities: What are the opportunities available to pursue?

Threats: What are the potential threats to that course of action?

Strengths: What are our current strengths and what future strengths will we need to pursue these opportunities and avoid these threats?

Weaknesses: What are our current weaknesses and which areas are we going to need to build to pursue these opportunities and avoid these threats?

2. Then ask them to **create action points** which will help them achieve the goals identified in part 1 (being mindful of the weaknesses, threats identified) using the following GROW model:

	Goal	Reality	Options	Will (to take action)	
What?	1. What do you want to happen?	5. What is going on right now?	9. What options are available/have you considered?	13. With No. 11 in mind, what will you do now?	Strategy
Why?	2. Why do you want this to happen – minimum of three reasons?	6. Why does the current situation have to change? What happens if it doesn't?	10. Which is your preferred option and why?	14. Why is this the preferred approach?	Drive
How?	3. How will you make it happen?	7. How do you think the situation got to this point?	11. How are you going to implement it?	15. How will this progress to your goal (No. 1)?	Opportunity

By when?	4. By when will you have implemented this?	8. By when did you think change was in order?	12. By when will you notice results and what are you looking for?	16. By when (and by whom) will this action be taken?	Achievement
Possible concerns	*Note that this section does not need to be filled in, but if you have any areas of concern, noting them will help you remain aware of them, and ensure that progress, even via an alternative, can still be made.*				*Alternative action*
	Outcome *Collective understanding of the goal envisaged – ideally resulting in commitment from the group.*	*Outcome* *Collective understanding of the current reality and how it came to be – this can also help avoid it in future.*	*Outcome* *Collective commitment to the strategy chosen.*	*Outcome* *Collective commitment to the action plan and proactive movement.*	

3. Then outline specific actions for each group to take based on points 13–16 that they have identified.

These two exercises together will get them thinking not only of the problems they face or the goals they know are attainable, but also how to develop an effective action plan to achieve them. Do this enough and they will be on their own path to leadership.

So what about you? Simply be the Plan B?

When you have embedded the ability to learn, with the awareness that it is experience which is the most effective teacher (although intellectualisation and practical support are always helpful), your role becomes one of *guidance*. You become 'Plan B' while encouraging 'Plan A'!

All this means is, when your teams do ask you for input – which they are likely do so simply because you are their leader – state what you have done or might do, but be clear that this is only one possible way.

You are no longer 'nudging' them to your solution, but have instead given them the process through which they can identify their own and feed it back to you.

What the experienced leader can offer their team or mentee (without suppressing them) is the teaching of the thought process rather than the possible solutions.

Try this

Rather than even suggesting possible ways of solving the matter raised, tell them how you might approach the problem.

Using a training example, when asked how to structure a training session, I suggested that the learner think about the outcome and how to get there, rather than teach the 'four-phase lesson plan', e.g.

- Engage curiosity/starter activity
- Teach the key message
- Self-directed learning activity
- Plenary/reflection (Brain Based Learning, Clapper, 2014).

This way the person asking may devise or find their own methods, but your experience gives them a jump start on the way in which to approach the task.

There is a difference between embedding hard skills and soft ones

Resilience, like many elements of leadership, is not a 'hard skill' (like riding a bike) that you can just learn and move on from. It is knowing that you can approach problems that don't yet have solutions, and do so with confidence. It is the ability to know that you have the strength and ability to bounce back (and sometimes bounce higher) from whatever you are in. It is faith that you will achieve if you put in the effort. It is being aware of who to ask, and actually asking. It is being innovative, or path carving – even when there is no map. It is saving your strength for the battles worth fighting – not getting caught up in petty squabbles that use up your valuable energy. Finally it is being grateful for what you have just because you have it. Resilience is about knowing you can – and will – find a way.

Those skills are harnessed and inspired. They can be nurtured and guided, especially by the brilliant and experienced leader – however, they cannot simply be taught.

END-OF-CHAPTER TOOLKIT

ADOPT Resilience now

Act

If you can identify something you are passionate about, see if
you can find a way to include it in your daily life – this may
be professional or personal or both. You can sometimes be
the best advocate by *doing* rather than talking about it. Even
if you are a strong orator, or influencer, it is often by watching
you that others realise it is possible.

> *This week:* Do one thing that you are passionate about –
> and then try and repeat it the next day, and the next . . .

Deal

It's never too late to make changes – even if you have been
doing things in a particular way, and you only now begin to
question its effectiveness. You may find that you need to
work that little bit harder to make your new practices stick,
and others may be surprised at your new behaviours.
However, if you are confident in taking a different approach,
it is better to start it now, than later, or not at all! The impact
of the change will be the same at any point, but the ease at
which *you* can adapt may lessen.

> *This week: If you have been inspired to do something
> differently, do it. Then reflect on it in a couple of weeks to see
> how it went.*

Optimise

Notice something special in your team? Perhaps it's a hobby
or an interest or something unrelated to the organisation,

but that could be helpful or interesting to others – invite them to talk about it or even to start an organisational club.

> *This week:* Be observant. Your best assets are the people around you. By recognising something they may not have realised could make a positive difference you are not only offering the opportunity to others to benefit, but acknowledging someone in a way that they might not expect.

Prepare

Remember that resilience is not about 'What would you do if you knew you couldn't fail?', but rather 'What would you do if you knew the effort would be worth it?'. Anything worth having takes work, but as well as obstacles or setbacks there are likely to be allies, support, easy wins and a sense of accomplishment on the journey.

> *This week:* You know there are no quick fixes, but you and your team are building the confidence to know that you will find a way. Even failures can be learned from. So if you want it, take that step.

Thrive

When you have a team that is capable of finding the answers – because you have been able to set up their environment to support their *learning* – the success outcomes are limitless. Seek to nurture rather than 'teach'.

> *This week:* Try and encourage your teams to take ownership of something they are confident in and perhaps ask them to offer feedback at a team briefing. Small steps are sometimes the best way to embed confidence, supporting all the other work you are doing.

Notes

What I did	Date

Reflection (at a later date)

How have my thoughts changed now?

References

Bloom, B. S., Engelhart, M. D., Furst, E. J., Hill, W. H. and Krathwohl, D. R. (1956) *Taxonomy of Educational Objectives: The classification of educational goals*. Handbook I: Cognitive domain. Longmans.

Clapper, T. C. (2014) Situational interest and instructional design: A guide for simulation facilitators. *Simulation & Gaming*, Vol. 45, No. 2, 167–182 https://www.researchgate.net/figure/Brain-based-learning-four-phase-lesson-plan_fig1_259891007 (accessed May 2020).

Cleese, J. and Booth, C. (1998) *The Complete Fawlty Towers*. Methuen Humour.

Eck, J. E. (2010) Places and the crime triangle. In F. T. Cullen and P. Wilcox (eds) *Encyclopedia of Criminological Theory*. SAGE Publications Inc.

Faulkner, M. (2018) *Surviving Leadership* https://survivingleadership.blog/2018/07/31/the-power-and-danger-of-being-liked/ (accessed May 2020).

Morgan, P. (2011) *Rush*. Screenplay http://www.screenplaydb.com/film/scripts/rush/ (accessed May 2020).

Shakespeare, W. (1623) *The Tragedy of Macbeth*. First Folio.

5
Establish a responsive network

Who is in your network?

Your initial thoughts may include 'clients', 'stakeholders', 'my team', the organisation as a whole . . . Yes, they are important, but your surrounding community – the people who live and work in your area – are as important. Perhaps their custom contributes to the longevity of your business, perhaps the schools and universities are producing future workers, perhaps you can collaborate with local contribution to make a broader impact on society as a whole.

Recruitment for a team is a carefully thought through process. When scaling this up to form a responsive community, it is an even more important task. Too often organisations wishing to 'give back' will make sweeping claims about 'bringing in work opportunities', but unless the community is equipped, those opportunities will at best be lost or at worst require extra intervention which can come at a cost of time, finance and even resentment.

This chapter encourages you to think of your organisation in terms of the broader network. This will include your immediate teams, your clients, but also all those with whom you collaborate or seek to support and include. Your network as a *whole* contributes to your strength. There may be new positive connections to be formed, or perhaps there are some where your paths no longer intertwine. Either way, your success may be affected – so be aware of who is around you, as well as yourself.

> Even if you feel someone is doing you a favour, always remember, you probably made them a good offer. Think as equals

Ask yourself

If you wanted to involve your local community in a new project, what elements would you outsource?

For each of those elements ask yourself:

- Does the organisation have the resources (materials, staffing, finances, training, etc.) to cope with the full demand of the project?

- In which areas are they lacking?

- How can my organisation help them meet the demand in future so that they can be immediately employed?

- For now, which elements can I reasonably outsource?

At the very basic level, universities such as Brunel, Northampton, Essex and Bradford, to name just a few where I have had the privilege of experiencing their work personally, have facilities such as hotels, conference centres, arts centres and restaurants which form part of the work experience for students studying hospitality, marketing, theatre and so on. Students are encouraged to not only train within these establishments, but to initiate and run their own events and projects so as to gain experience in an environment where support is readily available should they need it. Many vocational degrees such as Nursing and Teaching also value the importance of 'in situ' training.

However, to truly build a community, as important as having the necessary skills is motivating the desire to remain within that same community, thus retaining the talent you have so carefully nurtured.

This requires more collaboration.

Ask others

- If you are in a position to be able to offer training or opportunities for experience, can you find out from neighbouring businesses what sort of skills would be the most effective to nurture?
- How can you collaborate with other businesses in order to build a community that can be responsive to both immediate and future needs?

Competition or collaboration?

Competition has always been a factor in economic growth (Office of Fair Trading, 2019). Businesses need to increase their own efficiency in order to retain market share, and with that cost advantage (and possibly the less productive firms exiting the market), that business can differentiate their products and continue to generate revenue.

Can this long-held, successful approach to business sit with the collaboration needed to build a community?

Possibly.

In *The Leader's Guide to Mindfulness* I discussed the value of three different types of innovation proposed by Timms (2018):

▌ Core

▌ Adjacent

▌ Disruptive.

Innovation at the core is the development of something already common to the business – an example may be the 'differentiation' of product as in the opening paragraph of this section.

Adjacent innovation is the ability to draw from the skills of others within the environment in order to develop something new.

Disruptive innovation is the development of something completely novel not only to the business, but perhaps to the city, the country or even the world.

It is adjacent innovation that may be the most conducive to growth as a community.

Ask yourself

▌ When might it be more cost- or resource-effective to engage the skills of others in the community?

▌ How can I encourage my teams to reach out to others within our network?

A concern for teams (especially non-budget holders) can be – how do I fund a collaboration?

Draw up a list of organisations you can collaborate with to include their contact details and budget considerations, e.g. a collaborator on a retainer fee may perhaps be brought in more often, a case-by-case consultant may need a listing of their hourly or project rates.

Collaborators	Contact details	Financial basis for engagement

Avoiding 'decision by committee'

A potential concern to be mindful of when collaborating is who is responsible for what. This is especially important when a sense of ownership is encouraged. Having a clear structure, not just for funding a collaboration, but outlining the remit of the engagement as well as the first point of contact and the person who takes sign-off responsibility, is also important.

Once you have defined the remit of collaboration for your teams, extend the structure on a project basis, e.g.

PROJECT	Collaborator(s) and expected contribution (including delivery dates if applicable)	Point of contact for collaborators	Final signatory

You do not need to give this document to collaborators or partners you are working with. It is most likely that their fee will have been agreed based on their expected contribution, often with their point of contact. But if your team keeps this structure in mind, it is a simple way to ensure everyone contributes as expected. As you engage with more collaborations, it is even likely that this table will become part of an habitual mindset.

It may be important to note at this point, that these methods of defining structure are open to adaptation or change. It is not that I wish you to define your working in *my* way, but rather that you *define your working* – which is especially important as your organisation grows. This may be easier for those used to working within hierarchy, but no matter how flat a structure you wish to employ, it is nonetheless important that you have a structure.

Why is a structure important?

Simply because boundaries are important.

> *'When the common soldiers are too strong and their officers too weak, the result is insubordination. When the officers are too strong and the common soldiers too weak, the result is collapse. When the higher officers are angry and insubordinate, and on meeting the enemy give battle on their own account from a feeling of resentment, before the commander-in-chief can tell whether or no he is in a position to fight, the result is ruin. When the general is weak and without authority; when his orders are not clear and distinct; when there are no fixes duties assigned to officers and men, and the ranks are formed in a slovenly haphazard manner, the result is utter disorganization.'*
>
> Sun Tzu (1910), *The Art of War*.

Thankfully we are not talking leadership on the battlefield, but much can be learned. In doing so, I contrast this with my book on mindfulness.[9] Within that, I refer to my grandfather's Buddhist teachings about leadership through teaching, emphasising the key messages that:

> *'Character and steadiness . . .'* of a leader *'. . . will do more . . . than cleverness'*
> Assist those *'. . . evolving more gradually than you . . .'*
> *'. . . do not look altogether to wisdom, ability or character, but partly also to manners, to those who can get on well with others.'*
>
> (Seet, 1951 cited by Tang, 2018).

In *The Leader's Guide to Mindfulness* the focus is greatly on the importance of building a solid foundation in oneself and nurturing the same within your team. This is often done best through kindness and reflective practice. However, too much

---

[9] *The Leader's Guide to Mindfulness* (2018) is part of the Pearson *Leader's Guide* series and is the second of my titles.

of this and you may have the most enlightened team who does little, or the team formation is lost which can result in confusion . . . and again potential inaction.

It is important to have structure and direction as well as compassion and authenticity – but the latter is only the beginning, the second part is that it needs to be channelled to get things done well. As I said in the introduction, mindfulness calms you – resilience will arm you.

Tiedens and Zitek reviewed previous research on employee opinion of hierarchy and found that it significantly made people feel more comfortable. Egalitarian structures largely '. . . did not make sense' and '. . . could be messy'. Even colloquially we like to know where we stand in relationships, and the research suggests that this is because this makes it easier to '. . . know what is expected' and '. . . how to act' (Tiedens and Zitek, 2012, cited in Greenberg, 2012).

> **Whether your organisational structure is hierarchical or flat, ask yourself**
>
> *Are my team aware of the lines of communication for requesting what they need?*
>
> *Are my team aware of their remit:*
>
> ▎ *within their role*
>
> ▎ *within a project.*
>
> *If not – make this clear.*

You don't need to do everything

In fact, you probably cannot do everything, because you are often able to do a few things well. Saying that, it doesn't hurt to appreciate that having a broad knowledge of many skills has a place as well, and such breadth is particularly valuable in a time of crisis.

I've had the phrase 'Jack of all trades' levelled at me for many years – often as a bit of an insult. (What my biography doesn't say, beyond my current work, is that I also have degrees in Law, History, Teaching, Business, and professional qualifications in Aerobics, Drama, Acting and Lifeguarding. My career has taken me from a village primary school (which was probably my toughest gig) to the set of James Bond (*Spectre*), via work in Advertising, PR and many years of directing and producing community theatre. I am hugely lucky to have had so many opportunities to learn, and working through a number of job roles has meant I have a wide understanding of organisational styles – what works, what doesn't and where I fit in. I've never regretted having an eclectic background. Producing theatre means I can manage projects, and manage different skills sets, plus it has given me insights into nuance and body language that cannot be taught; I credit Law for my ability to write, whether that's articles, books or even letters of complaints and reviews(!); and psychology is my passion. However, I do not need to be managing a production to manage effectively, every skill is transferrable – *but you must recognise that.* Further, 'Jack of all trades' is only the *first* half of that phrase.)

From Chapter 2, you will appreciate I am a co-operative board game player, which underpins this example with the game of Pandemic.[10] In this game, as a team of four you choose characters to eradicate a disease. We have always chosen specialist characters, e.g. 'The Medic', 'The Quarantine Expert', 'The Researcher', 'Dispatcher', all of whom have 'special abilities' that can specifically help you achieve your goals. For example, the Medic can 'treat' disease more efficiently, the 'Dispatcher' can move your character places, and so on. In Legacy Season 1 we were given the option of a more unusual role 'The Generalist'. Her only power being 'one extra turn'.

Would you choose her?

---

[10]Matt Leacock, Z-Man Games.

The specialists were far more useful, and at the end of every game we lost we said: 'If only we'd had that extra turn'. Every single time.

The thing about 'Legacy' is that it is ongoing, which means your characters, should you wish, can be 'upgraded'. They can be given extra abilities, extra skills, extra advantages; and it was after the fourth game we lost, taking us mid-way into the campaign, when we collectively realised: 'We should have played The Generalist from the start and upgraded her.'

Of course it was a bit too late in our Pandemic campaign by that point.

But it's not too late for organisations.

In training I always teach that having transferrable skills is essential. It means you can turn your hand to anything – as long as you recognise the essence of the skill which is needed. If, on top of that, you have (like my husband) an innate ability to learn and be at about 70% proficiency at the start of picking something up compared with someone who takes longer, but can then achieve 99%, you are extremely valuable. Your 'Generalist' ability can be deployed wherever there is an up to 70% gap in the chain.

Within the global pandemic of 2020, some of the workforce had to 'shield', others were furloughed. This reduced the amount of available skill. If you could do other jobs – or learn to do them – you became an extremely valuable asset. This was the time where understudies became stars.

Try this

It is perhaps possible to learn from Pandemic Legacy too. While it is wonderful to have someone who can fill that gap and then be redeployed, it is also helpful to keep upgrading the role. If your Generalist wishes to specialise, give them

➤

the opportunity. It may mean they are able to fill fewer gaps, but being mindful of the needs of your team encourages loyalty. However, in times of crisis, it is as wise to remind the Generalist of their value – it is often at this point that their ability to adapt means they can seize the opportunity to be the star.

▌ Identify any 'Generalists' in your team (people skilled in a number of different areas).

▌ If the situation allows, recognise their ability and ask them if they would like to specialise in any particular area (perhaps you can offer a set choice) – then give them the means to do so, e.g. assigning them specifically in that area to a project.

▌ Identify any specialists in your team and ask them what they might like to develop as a secondary area (again perhaps offering a pre-chosen selection).

. . . so as to the phrase: Jack of all trades, master of none . . . The second part reads: *Is oftimes better than master of one.*

Outsourcing is helpful too (but structure is again the key).

Ask yourself

You have the opportunity to take on a lucrative project, but do not have the skills set to hand. How will you accept it?

If there is no-one in your team and it would not be cost and/ or time efficient to train them, then consider who you might collaborate with – *and on what basis.*

Structure is essential here, to avoid poaching or usurping of business, or any confusion with the client as to who they are instructing. If you already have a working team structure, it is much easier to incorporate a contractor.

To help with outsourcing, find out

▌ If there are field-based or government initiatives which may contribute to your work.

▌ Who your immediate community is and what skills lie within it.

▌ What directions your field may grow within in future, and what you need to do to stay competitive or break new ground.

. . . then begin to reach out to connect.

Be an organisation where 'not knowing' is ok

Following on from the point above, make it ok to know you are less able at something than someone else, and be comfortable asking for training, or giving the job to them to do.

Ask yourself (and your team)

What skills do you feel you are lacking?

Out of these which do you feel it would be beneficial to learn – and what opportunities are there to get that training?

Out of the ones where you do not feel it beneficial to learn, whom do you know who would be able to fill that gap?

While this seems quite a simple task, many people are afraid of admitting they do not know something. For some it may be helpful for them to reflect on whether what they do not know will be important in their field should their circumstances change, or whether they are comfortable collaborating with others when that skill is needed. It is arguable that the most effective leaders know in principle how most elements of their job should be done, even if they do not have the ability – or time – to do it all; but thinking you 'have to do it all' is not a helpful position to hold. The leader – or team member – who tries to keep everything to themselves misses out on empowering their teams and often does not do the multitude of jobs to the best of their ability. Worse still, this may result in team members also hoarding their work for fear of sharing.

Try this

This is an exercise adapted from that presented by Mike Burrows at the Project Management Conference, Athens, 2017.

You need:

  1 × chart per group (3–5 players)

  1 × dice

  3–5 × little sticky notes (ideally in different colours).

Instructions: Each person writes their name on five sticky notes, numbering them 1–5.

The object of the game is to move all sticky notes across each column on the board to the 'complete' pile.

Rules: You take it in turns and throw the dice to move.

If you get an odd number 1, 3, 5 you may EITHER start a new task (i.e. bring it onto the board), or progress a task you have already started along one column.

If you get an even number 2, 4, 6 you CANNOT progress a task you have already started, but you CAN start a new task, or progress someone else's started task.

THE BOARD

START	STAGE 1	STAGE 2	STAGE 3	COMPLETION

As you watch teams play you will most likely notice that there will be a backlog because people will keep starting new tasks when they get an even number. (Only teams that help each other will be clearing the board.) After about 5-6 minutes, or when you see the backlog, introduce a new rule:

New rule: You Can Never Have More Than Three Tasks in Each Column

Without overtly telling the teams to help each other, they will start moving each other's tasks to the next column to follow the rule – this means that if they cannot do their own work, they will often 'offer to help'.

➤

This will enable you to open a discussion on the importance of collaboration.

Note also that the roll of the dice is used because of the element of unpredictability – very much like life. What if the even number means that you have to 'sign off' (or help) someone else get their work done? Rather than just thinking of your own work, this game enables you to see the whole process of the project as a team effort.

Your vision of the future must also consider your present

In the search for a collaborative and responsive network, it is important not just to have the practicalities in place (e.g. the training, the tools and other elements previously discussed in this chapter), but also the commitment from all involved.

Unfortunately, with the growth of a 'swipe right or left' culture, society becoming more remote, and 'project-based' lifestyles being consistent in their inconsistency, loyalty and reciprocation may suffer. As you seek success, also remember to acknowledge and appreciate what you have.

Try this

1. Identify the vision of your future (e.g. what will you be doing, how will you be making an impact?).
2. Identify who will help you achieve this.

Both lists are important, but it can sometimes be easier to push for the first without always recognising the second. Can you, every time you pursue a wonderful opportunity in the first, make sure you replenish the second? For example, for every new connection, make sure you have acknowledged and thanked an old one.

Prioritising and choosing wisely where to spend your efforts is an essential part of growth.

END-OF-CHAPTER TOOLKIT

ADOPT Resilience now

Act

Remember your priorities lie with the present as well as the future.

> *This week:* Identify the people you value in your team. Recognise and thank them for their contribution. It doesn't need to be a long speech nor a big deal, just a simple word of appreciation.

Deal

Spend some time thinking about the future impact you wish your organisation to make, and what skills you will need in order to achieve that in a sustainable, yet competitive manner.

Then: Take at least one action to start filling any skills gap, e.g. through reaching out to other networks, or identifying who in your current network could make an effective collaboration.

Optimise

Make sure your efforts are directed and optimised. While resilience is as much about being able to 'go back to the drawing board' if need be, if you are going to put effort in to make changes it may as well be as useful as possible! The reason why people often find themselves repeating things

➤

(as well as events occurring out of their control), is because a moment thinking the plan through may save time in the execution. While you can only consider things that are reasonably foreseeable, that is still better than rushing forward headlong in the wind simply because you 'got inspired'. Inspiration is a wonderful thing, and sometimes you DO have to pounce on opportunities, but considered action may be even more effective.

> *This week:* Think about that 'vision of the future' so that your mind is primed to look at the areas of opportunity that are most helpful to your progress.

Prepare

If you are going to collaborate, be aware of the options around you. To return to Sun Tzu's *'Art of War'*, part of a general's success is not only knowing his character, but also knowing the opposition, and the environment.

> *This week:* Be aware of what resources surround you. Notice how your neighbouring organisations function, what their aims or agendas are, and the behaviours of the staff members they bring in. Look also beyond the immediate environment to the collaborative opportunities beyond that, as well as much closer – to the potential you have in your own organisation. Think also about how any collaboration is to be structured so that if or when the time comes, you are ready.

Thrive

Fan the flame of passion within your work by reminding yourself what you love about what you do. Research by Achor *et al.* (2018) shows that people are often motivated by meaningful work, so remember what brought you to your profession, and check that this is still part of your working day.

This week: Make a conscious effort to do something every day within your work that you love. If you came to your role because you love connecting with people, connect; if you came because of the positive impact you make – find a way of acknowledging and celebrating that. Whatever it is that drew you in can get lost between the daily grind or rush unless you make time to remember its presence. Being mindful of this will help keep you focused ESPECIALLY as you continue to grow and collaborate – as it means your direction remains clear. Note that it is ok if your direction changes, as long as you always have a conscious awareness of the ultimate goal.

Try this simple act of acknowledgment right now: One of the things I love about my work is . . . ; and today I am looking forward to . . .

Try and get your team to do that too.

Notes

What I did	Date

Reflection (at a later date)

How have my thoughts changed now?

References

Achor, S., Reece, A., Rosen Kellerman, G. and Robichaux,
A. (2018) 9 out of 10 people are willing to earn less money to
do more-meaningful work. *Harvard Business Review* https://
hbr.org/2018/11/9-out-of-10-people-are-willing-to-earn-less-
money-to-do-more-meaningful-work (accessed May 2020).

Burrows, M. (2017) Workshop at the Project Management
Conference, Athens 2017 @asplake; agendashift.com/mike

Office of Fair Trading (2019) https://www.gov.uk/government/
speeches/competition-policy-and-economic-growth-principles-and-
practice (accessed September 2020).

Tang, A. (2018) *The Leader's Guide to Mindfulness.*
Pearson.

Tiedens, L. Z. and Zitek, E. M. (2012) cited in Greenberg, S. (2012) Building Organizations that Work, *Insights by Stanford Business* https://www.gsb.stanford.edu/insights/building-organizations-work

Timms, P. (2018) cited by Tang, A. (2018) *The Leader's Guide to Mindfulness.* Pearson.

Tzu, S. (1910) *The Art of War* https://sites.ualberta.ca/~enoch/Readings/The_Art_Of_War.pdf (accessed May 2020).

6 Be authentic

Too often we lose ourselves in our 'adaptive' self. This is the self which is shaped by the expectations, the 'shoulds' and the structures of the things we do and the roles we play. However, if you also engage with your authentic self, not only will this give you a sense of wholeness, but achieving that blend between your work role and your life may enhance your leadership professionally, and your impact personally. A strong 'adaptive self' is a common issue which arises with my coaching clients – they have spent so long within a role professionally (or socially, e.g. 'parent') they are not always sure who they are, and on top of that worry what others will say should they suddenly do something perceived to be 'out of character'.

The struggle with authenticity seems to rest in the issue of 'face'. . . or perhaps 'dignity', or perhaps 'professionalism'. Note that permission to be authentic does not mean permission to hurt others, or absolve you of accountability for the consequences of your behaviour choices. It means exploring 'you' as an holistic person – the actor as well as the role you play – the substance behind the front.

The question of 'face'

'Saving face' (Matsumoto, 2020) is more often related to Eastern cultures (notably Chinese and Japanese). In

Japanese the phrase 'kao o tateru' means to 'give face' – i.e. proffer dignity to someone such as a boss, or an elder; and 'mentsu wo tamotsu' which means 'save face' – retaining of one's reputation or standing in the eyes of others.

The concept is not alien to the Western World, the difference is that 'face' in Chinese and Japanese culture is more related to social harmony; whereas in the UK and America, it is more about personal or individual integrity and the truth. (Having been brought up in a fundamentally Eastern (Chinese–Malay) household, but within the UK, I have often struggled with which 'face' I need to save and give!)

Sociologically 'Japanese (and Chinese and Malay) culture has downplayed the concept of the individual . . . with the emphasis on the collective, the sense of self blurred so much that it practically didn't exist . . . Western cultures tend to focus on the individual as an independent self-reliant being . . . where misbehaviour is often blamed on lack of self-esteem'.

What is not often discussed, however, is that there is an acute awareness (conscious or otherwise) in both cultures of the problem with one singular approach to upbringing. The Japanese and Chinese may 'save and give face' to preserve the harmony at work, but then 'let loose' when among friends at the end of the day; in the UK and USA, a potential sensitive or caring side may be hidden because of the desire to present a strong self.

As a leader, you will always be playing some sort of game. You will be donning some sort of costume. Just make sure you know when it comes off, who you are underneath. I will discuss this further under the section 'Month 2: Emotional labour'.

Yet, the ability to blend the personal and professional – knowing your role, but acting authentically within it – if managed well, will not undermine your leadership persona, but unlock another level with which you can interact and influence.

Therefore, this is my challenge to you.

Your challenge

This chapter offers you 12 ways in which you can explore who you are as a person and apply it to your leadership. I've set them out so that you can work on one a month, but there's nothing to stop you trying them all out together, repeating what works and discarding the rest – whatever you prefer – each is simply a development prompt. It's a little like self-coaching.

So, are you ready for a year of being authentic?

Month 1: Live your VITALS

Reflect

Think back to the exercise in Chapter 1 – 'living your VITALS'. If you are not reading this in one sitting, take a moment to reflect now over whether, since first encountering the exercise, you have been able to live them at all. If you have, well done – what did you find particularly easy and why? If you haven't, why not?

As a reminder your 'VITALS' – so named because they are as important to life as oxygen and a heartbeat – include your Values, Interests, (preferred) Temperament, Around-the-clock rhythm (e.g. being a morning/evening person), Life (or meaningful) goals and expressing your known Strengths. If you are able to engage with at least one of them each day it is likely you will feel more grounded and at ease with who you are and what you are doing. If you are constantly at odds with your VITALS, you are likely to feel a constant sense of unease as you struggle – consciously or otherwise – to fit into a role that is unnatural to you . . . even if you manage that 'fit' successfully.

While you may be extremely successful 'playing a role', I ask you to consider the following coaching question: *Would the younger version of you be happy with you as a role model?*

The reason I frame the question this way (rather than the more conventional 'Would the younger you be proud of who you are now?') is because you may have achieved things that the younger you may not even have known would exist. And, more importantly, the fundamental question beyond achievements – *are you the person you hoped you would be – the person you can respect and love*? Are you the role model you would like for those around you?

How can you expect others to engage authentically if you are always just 'playing the game' or 'playing the part'? And, if you do not feel complete within yourself, is this really what you want for others, no matter how successful you have become?

Authenticity is not about disregarding the need for professionalism, it is about appreciating there is more to you than your job. This idea is explored in more depth in 'Month 2'.

> *This month:* Try to do one thing daily within at least one of the VITALS you have identified. Reflect on how that makes you feel.

Month 2: Focus on your use of emotional labour

Emotional labour was defined by Arlie Russell Hochschild in 1983 as a socially constructed behaviour where a service worker manages his or her '. . . feelings to create a publicly observable facial and bodily display . . . This kind of labour calls for a coordination of mind and feeling, and it sometimes draws on a source of self that we honour as deep and integral to our individuality' (Hochschild, 2003).

For Hochschild, emotional labour was constructed as the outward display of emotion that fits organisational norms. Sometimes, she proposed, those 'norms' are defined by display rules that performers of emotional labour might share (e.g. a nurse is supposed to present as an approachable and sympathetic person). With the number of titles on leadership behaviour, it is also clear that there is an expectation for a leader to be many things to many people!

The most prominent argument throughout Hochschild's work is the negative consequences of emotional labour performance – the alienation of the worker from their own feelings. For the leader who is expected to be motivating, as well as a visionary, as well as supportive, direct, efficient, aggressive (as needed), and be able to adapt as the situation arises, this can also result in a similar discord between professional and personal feelings; the constant *display* of one emotion, e.g. happiness, in contrast to a different internal feeling, means 'There is a cost to emotional work' (Hochschild, 2003). As well as losing your sense of self, perhaps you may hold a personal resentment in offering a perceived *ungrateful* team member a smile and 'withdraw' from emotional labour, or your 'easy going' performance (your 'leadership character') may become 'phony or insincere'.

Ask yourself

How often do you find yourself speaking 'professionally' rather than expressing how you really feel?

When this happens, do you have an opportunity to express your true feelings?

Note that while it is common to express (or vent) one's personal frustration to a spouse or other loved one, this is not always the best person to choose. A loved one simply wants what is best for you – and often is consumed with their own concerns – as such you may not receive the level of support you need in managing the exhaustion of the emotional labour of leadership.

Find out

Are there any coaching or mentoring opportunities available to you?

Are there others in a similar position who you can seek support from?

It is not always helpful to express your frustrations to your team, even if you are on friendly terms with them; if they like you it may cloud their own view of their relationship with the organisation. Also, they are not there as your support . . . if nothing else, it is above their pay grade to deal with your issues! Further, they, like a loved one, may also simply not have the experience to help solve what you are going through. Therefore either the opportunity to talk things through to find a solution or seek advice from others with the requisite experience will be of most help.

> *This month*: Reflect on your use of emotional labour, and identify the ways that will help you express your own feelings. After all, if you continually contain the anxieties of others, like a glass, if you have no outlet, you cease to function as a useful container!

Month 3: Live consciously

Over the Christmas period I decided to give my friends the 'gift of thought'. In lieu of gifts I gave them money, but with the explicit instruction to spend it consciously. This resulted in some lovely outcomes – family outings, donations to important personal courses, and treats for oneself and others. Most importantly it was not what they did with the money that mattered, it was that they thought about it. They all reported feeling happier with their spending because they had overtly ruminated on it, and they also said that it made them think more about their other purchases . . . helpful at a time when habitual over-spending is common!

Living authentically is not about 'liking' everything you have to do, but it is about knowing you have conscious choice in doing it. So often, especially when you are experienced in your job, your life functions on 'auto pilot'. You do not have to change anything you do, but I would like you to see if being aware that you are doing it makes a difference to your actions.

This is especially significant if you are trying to make changes. It is very easy to write off a diet by the automatic thought: 'I have to eat X with a client'. However, thinking consciously may make you aware of other potential options.

This month:

▌ Make a mental note when you are enjoying part of your work, and when you are not . . . then see if you can engage in the bits you enjoy more, and find something positive in the elements that are less palatable.

▌ Consciously choose the behaviours you show others. You may even find that when you are aware you are choosing to act in a certain way, you have other options available that may be more successful on that specific occasion.

Month 4: Curate your life (Martin Turner, 2019, www.mutatiocoach.com)

Note that this exercise can be done hypothetically with clients, teams, or personal friendships.

> **Ask yourself**
>
> When, where, and with whom do you find you are most at ease? Why?
>
> What would happen if you were to say what you wanted to say, or voiced how you feel with other (specific) people?
>
> Why are you less 'authentic' with them?

Editing your relationships is ok!

The statement 'The people you start the year with are not always the same ones you end it with' is often met with sadness and regret. Of course the pain of bereavement cannot be ignored within those words, but what is often meant is that friendships and relationships change.

The most empowering thing to realise is that you choose relationships, they do not choose you!

What if I have too much choice?

All the more reason to be wise!

If you are blessed with the traits that draw people to you – e.g. beauty, kindness, generosity, talent – you may have a multitude of people wanting to be by your side. This will often be true of charismatic leaders. *Never forget that your time and energy are valuable (and often finite) resources – spend them wisely!*

Choose relationships like clothing. BUT REAL CLOTHING – not the idea in your head, nor the look on the model. Choose clothing that you will wear because it fits you, suits you and enhances you, and then look after THOSE clothes!

It's not ghosting if you're both absent!

It takes two to put the effort into a relationship – and this includes clients. We all have commitments and priorities that we need to attend to, and the intensity that might have been afforded to us when we were younger is no longer attainable. But, as all reflective processes channel you, look at the *quality* of the contact.

Ask yourself

▌ How do you envision a relationship that will make you happy? (Unfortunately, you will not be able to put a specific person there, because their choice is always their own, but you can have an idea of the type of person you seek.) This may be the type of client you want to work with, or the type of person you want in your team – as well as a personal friendship.

▌ Set out what values you want in that person, and what you are not willing to accept.

▌ Set out what values you want them to recognise in you.

THEN focus on living your Values and make your choices accordingly.

This month: Look carefully at your relationships (including those with your teams and clients).

Ask yourself

▌ Which ones are reciprocal?

▌ Which ones bring me joy?

▌ Which ones encourage honesty?

▌ Which ones can I rely on?

and most importantly

▌ Which ones are with people I respect for their own values and actions? (Which ones do I actively want to choose?)

Month 5: Know your WHY

What brought you to this job?

Are you still engaging in that?

So often people come to a role because they want to engage in something. As they gain experience, improve at their job and achieve promotion, the tasks which brought them to their jobs seem to drift further away. This is a common dilemma for headteachers, senior clinicians and others who now find their day consumed with more administrative and organisational detail rather than at the coal face of making a difference.

It is important to realise that in a leadership role you are still making a difference. You are firstly empowering your team to best help the people you wanted to help in the first instance; you may also be helping clients to make their own mark on the world. With the changes and growth in technology and materials accessible to you, you can make a greater impact now than you ever imagined you could when you first applied for the job!

▌ What is meaningful to you about your job?

▌ What are the ways in which your role has changed?

▌ What do these changes now allow you to do?

Being authentic is not about clinging to a romanticised past, but using the present and future to continue what inspired you in the first instance.

This month: Find the ways in which it's 'worth it'.

When you look around, do you see whatever it was that brought you to the job in the first instance?

If you do, it's worth it. What you see, especially if you have been in your role for some time is as much a reflection of you and your actions as it is on your environment.

If, on the other hand, you are constantly questioning 'Why do I bother?' or you notice that you go to great efforts that are often not returned; or maybe you feel like people seem to see you only when it suits them, then maybe it's time to edit your life (see last month!).

Month 6: Be honest about your strengths and weaknesses

Resilience is about growth and regeneration rather than removal of the past. Once you have authentic honesty as a leader, you then use that same approach to gain an understanding of the environment in which you are operating, and the cultural impacts within it as well. History has horrible atrocities that we would prefer to forget, they are a part of who we are – we remember in order to avoid future occurrences, but also because they have shaped us and those around us, with whom our now hugely connected world allows us to collaborate.

Note your habitual responses

Usually this is a thought process set down in childhood which drives us to behave in a certain way. Such beliefs can include:

- You're so pretty
- You're special
- You're so clever
- You're so brave.

Or

▌ You're ugly

▌ You'll never succeed

▌ You're too emotional.

The lists are endless, but they will all include something which people close to you have repeated for some time, and there will be an element of truth to them. However, where this can askew your behaviour is when you start believing that is the only thing that you amount to.

If you have always been told that you are 'a winner', rather than stop and think how the situation ended up at the litigious point in the first place, you may glory more in a win at all costs.

If told 'you're pretty', rather than focus on why people may not take you as seriously as you like, you may prefer to post a saucy picture and tell everyone you're beautiful.

If told 'you're a success', rather than appreciate the moment of peace to recharge with who and what matters, you may be looking for the next passion project to figurehead for the troops.

If you've always had to rely on yourself, rather than question why someone responded abruptly, you shut down and remind yourself it's they who have the problem.

This is not authentic, this is habitual! Those habits, those go-to responses, have been helpful in getting you through, perhaps at times when you have felt or been completely alone. But you are likely not in that exact situation anymore. That response – your ability to argue and succeed; your winning smile; your passionate address; your 'talk to the hand' – is effective sometimes, and will continue to be. But you are much more than that.

This month:

See if you can recognise any habitual thought processes which contribute to your identity, then recondition the habit.

1. Take a moment to reflect on that situation – what were the links in the chain that led up to your response. What made you feel bad, sad, ashamed, upset, rejected . . . ?

2. Consider other courses of action you could have taken – not for right now, but next time, if you are able to catch yourself sooner (write them down if it helps)

Month 7: Be honest when asking for help

Ask yourself

When you ask for help, are you asking because you want to hear my opinion – or hear your own being validated?

If the latter – it becomes difficult to grow.

Find someone who can challenge you

This can be a coach, a friend, a partner, perhaps even what you read online, or a virtual support – a sort of human 'spirit guide' (guide for your spirit perhaps, to see it another way) and ideally someone whose opinion you respect, who asks the right questions and makes useful observations rather than tries to tell you what to do. If you are reflective, you are able to pinpoint when you feel a little derailed and your 'guide' can help you explore what you're feeling. If you are focused in one direction, it might mean you are losing sight of others – again, that guide can remind you to re-focus on your priorities while they are simply being 'overlooked' rather than falling into neglect. The key to this relationship, however, is *honesty*, and the drive to bring out the best in each other – *above any other agenda*.

> *This month*: actively seek feedback, and reflect on the following when you receive it:
>
> ▌ Who is saying it, and do they have any other agenda than my improvement?
>
> ▌ Do I want to change what they have identified? If not, why not? (As long as you can justify your reasons, it is ok not to change.)

Month 8: Look after yourself

Those that often need self-care the most are often the least forthcoming in engaging with it. Perhaps this is due to a misplaced sense of duty; perhaps there is a 'guilt' associated with 'doing nothing'. If you are that busy leader who multi-tasks, you may not always be offering your best, nor healthiest practice, and you are not modelling positive behaviour to your team.

These five simple tips will help you (and your teams) recognise when you (they) are feeling under pressure, and temper the effects:

▌ **Listen to your body (forget the 'experts')** No-one can ever be more of an expert on your body than you, so why do you so often ignore the signs when it is struggling? Becoming more aware of what triggers any of the stress responses mentioned can help you avoid them – or deal with them before they begin to get worrisome. Be pro-active rather than being forced to react at a later point.

▌ **Look after your body physically** With stress being a physiological response, physical care can be just as important as emotional and mental support for building resilience to stress. Eating sensibly, drinking water, going to the toilet when you need to, sleeping well and simple things such as taking breaks can help our bodies function better. After all, burning the candle at both ends to meet deadlines, or riding particularly busy times often asks a lot of your body – so you would do well to look after it.

▌**Find healthy means of enjoying adrenaline** For some of you 'stress' can be a motivator! However, rather than leaving things until the last minute, because you 'work better under pressure', consider doing the job early, and being able to improve on it nearer the deadline. Then find other (healthy) ways of getting that 'adrenaline rush' that you may crave.

▌**Practise gratitude** Even the most confident leader can get caught up in thoughts of what you 'should' have done, or 'could' be doing still. The practice of gratitude helps you focus on the here and now. Go on, right now – think of one thing you're grateful to have; and one person you are grateful to know.

▌**Add 'SPICES' to your life for flavour (Life & Parenting Coach, Sharon Lawton www.natural-flair.com)** Put the numbers 1–6 in a hat (or roll a dice) and each day, seek to engage with one area that allows you some self-care in the following categories:

1. Spiritual (e.g. meditation, deep breathing)

2. Physical (e.g. exercise)

3. Intellectual (e.g. a course, or a new skill)

4. Creative (e.g. a form of self-expression, writing, singing, dancing, gardening)

5. Emotional (e.g. a spa or a massage, or reflecting on what you are proud of)

6. Social (e.g. doing something with people who energise you).

This month: Find time to engage with any of the above five exercises at least once a week.

Month 9: It's ok to be a work in progress

As much as it would be lovely to win the lottery and go and live on an island paradise, most of us are in our roles for the long term. This means that while you are making changes, they do not all have to happen straight away.

> **Reflect**
>
> Think about a recent problem or situation you have faced.
>
> Ask yourself – what might you have told yourself last year?
>
> Acknowledge the change in your mind set.

Knowing you 'will try' is often as empowering as 'having done'

Perhaps you haven't 'saved the world', but you are in a field where you're making a difference to someone's life. Maybe you haven't travelled as far as you wanted, or achieved that award or mastered that skill – but there's still time and you are the sort of person who will try. Could it be that you feel fulfilled, but there seems to be a voice in your head telling you – 'do more' 'be more'?

Don't judge based on the outcome. Recognise the fact you can not only try, but that you have the strength to do so.

> *This month*: Note the number of times you make an effort.

Month 10: Ask yourself, honestly, are you REALLY missing out?

A relatively new psychological phenomenon really only entered research literature around 1996 – the advent of social media is FOMO – the Fear Of Missing Out. Psychologist William Schutz (1958) also stated that inclusion was a fundamental human need – as essential to us as food and water for survival.

To take the example of popular TV shows, *Game of Thrones*, *Eurovision*, Reality TV – anything in the shared sphere (made smaller through social media) gives us something to talk about – especially if those we see on a day-to-day basis (e.g. at work, or our friends) are watching it, otherwise we would have been left out. Or if you don't watch then you might have to avoid a whole sphere of contact until you've gotten up to date, and little else makes you feel more like a social pariah these days.

Ask yourself

In what areas do you fear 'isolation'? Do you engage in behaviours you do not enjoy simply because others are doing it?

Why is inclusion in those areas so important? What need does that fulfil?

Then spend time focusing on how that need may be met with a pursuit more suited to you. For example, if you wish to be included in a friendship group, rather than offer a reason related to work or even offering them an opportunity in order to spend time with them, ask them for a coffee!

This month: Focus on what needs you wish to be met, and find a way of meeting them that feels right for you:

If you want 'likes' – be with people who like you!

If you want connection – make time for your friends in real life. Bear in mind just because technology has made it easier to see what people are up to doesn't mean that will happen – nor will the 'Likes' if you do happen to 'trend' ever be as fulfilling as simply being with the people you love. Technology is a tool, not a way of life – no matter how much it feels otherwise.

Instead of using stories, e.g. 'I've got a "friend" who . . .', try and live your life honestly and express your truth.

Month 11: Think about how you want to be seen by others

Just as you judge others, you too are judged. Further, the Actor–Observer effect (Nisbett *et al.*, 1973) does not afford the person doing the judging (the observer) the same perspective as the actor. If you want to be perceived in a certain way, make sure you are living up to it.

To return to the idea of cultural preferences from the start of this chapter, the significance of your word is key to this point. There are some cultures where saying what immediately pacifies – rather than what is necessarily true – is the preferred choice over risking antagonism if the truth be told; for example, the airline who says 'The flight is slightly delayed', when they really mean 'This delay could last 4 hours'. A client I had also admitted in her cultural upbringing 'yes' often means 'we'll see'. None of this matters if you are happy to deal with the consequences of your word being perceived as insincere.

> *This month*: Reflect on what you are willing and unwilling to accept when it comes to trusting the reliability in others, and work so that you meet those standards. Being seen as unreliable or untrustworthy (whatever the 'good' reason) can undermine all your other positive traits. Everyone accepts that things 'go wrong', but when inconstancy is commonplace, ask yourself – is this really how I want to be perceived?

Month 12: Be more *you*

Try this

Look how far you've come.

Ask yourself:

- what does your ideal life look like?
- list your achievements both professionally and personally which contribute to that ideal.

You may notice you are already there!

Now focus on being better rather than 'good'

By recognising – and appreciating – what you have right, you may come to appreciate that you are already doing what you set out to do. Rather than choosing a dream, perhaps you are tweaking it, or seeking more of certain elements, or effecting change from an 'achieved' standpoint. When you can see that you are, it is even easier to grow.

> *This month*: Instead of a finite goal, look at where you are on your path to living your 'ideal' life, do *more* of the things that will support your goal, and strive to be *better* at those elements that are serving you well.

And try this affirmation: I am grateful for what I have, I am working to be better at, and am open to more of, what I love.

> When you add in more authenticity there is less room (or need) for pretence

END-OF-CHAPTER TOOLKIT

ADOPT Resilience now
(Your action points are those within this chapter!)

By being true to yourself, you begin to blend the professional with the personal. Through doing so you may discover broader choices in your responses, you may infuse your professional actions with the passion of what brought you to the job – in turn inspiring your team and your clients. You may feel more grounded.

Act

If something feels 'off kilter' recognise it by writing it down. You may not find what is troubling you right away, and therefore writing it down prevents you clogging your mind up trying to remember it, but through acknowledgement you are primed to be open to finding an explanation and later a solution for it.

Deal

If your change in behaviour is noted, it's ok to say you are experimenting with your own leadership development. It might even inspire others to do the same, especially when you achieve results.

Optimise

Utilise your best assets of your personal and professional life in both areas. I have a client who has learned to deal with a difficult school in the way she argues a legal case, and another who brings her passion for her job into the 'standard pitch' for new clients which suddenly elevates its effect.

Prepare

Know that authenticity is about honesty and that there *will* be areas you may not like, or even be ashamed of. Tell yourself that while you may not be proud of past behaviours, you will have had a reason for engaging in them, and no longer need to do so.

Thrive

Whatever stories you are telling yourself which may be preventing you from being truly, authentically, happy – remember they are only stories of which you are the narrator. One of the biggest barriers to authenticity is feelings of guilt or undeservedness. Remember when it comes to guilt that often you were not the only party involved and others must also take responsibility for their choices; when it comes to what is deserving, ask yourself – who is doing the judging?

As I said at the start of the chapter, I am giving you permission to be *you*.

Notes

What I did	Date

Reflection (at a later date)

How have my thoughts changed now?

References

Hochschild, A. R. (2003) *The Managed Heart*. University of California Press.

Lawton, S. (2020) *Energy Top Up* Show on *The Wellness League* www.natural-flair.com https://www.youtube.com/watch?v=dHE2qn6oFH4 (accessed May 2020).

Matsumoto, K. (2020) Face is everything in Japan. *TalkAbout Japan Blog* https://talkaboutjapan.com/save-face-in-japanese-culture/ (accessed May 2020).

Nisbett, R. E. Caputo, C., Legant, P. and Marecek, J. (1973) Behavior as seen by the actor and as seen by the observer. *Journal of Personality and Social Psychology,* Vol. 27, No. 2, 154–164.

Schutz, W. C. (1958) *FIRO: A three-dimensional theory of interpersonal behavior*. Rinehart.

Turner, M. (2019) Mutatio coaching session, The Timber Yard, December 2019 www.mutatiocoach.com

part

2

Shaping resilient organisations

Lay resilient foundations

The focus of Part 1 was on building resilience within the self and how that can work within your leadership role, or with your teams. Part 2 looks to scale that up to your organisation as a whole and beyond to the wider community and network wherein your organisation exists – and has the opportunity to thrive. The elements of building a 'resilient city' from the OECD (2020) act as a good reminder here.

Resilient cities (a community-based approach from the OECD)

'Resilient cities' are (re)built to withstand unpredictable environmental adversity. They are designed to the following urban planning principles to:

- attract and maintain courageous people (teams if taking an organisational mindset);
- harness drive and inspire collective passion within the community;
- nurture a network responsive to change;
- engage in mindful future planning;
- establish a culture that welcomes creativity and innovation;
- empower and structure so EVERYONE has authority and the knowledge to be responsive;

▌ utilise local resources and networks;

▌ propose values which include sustainability and growth.

These are all elements which we have explored in Part 1. Your task is now to apply what you have learned to strengthen your organisation.

Rebuilding anything brings its own obstacles

Remember, you are not starting from scratch. There will be habits, behaviours, preferences and methodologies that are commonplace. Minimal change is troublesome enough to implement when it is needed; in taking pro-active action, the benefits may not be recognised first.

It can be helpful to remember when one comes to rebuilding anything that similar principles can apply to the person, the team and the collective as to the architecture, so you may face these issues as you continue through this book.

▌ *There is often the importance of saving the facade (or saving face!).* This means that when faced with a challenge (even one within an exercise) that people are uncertain of, or one that makes them feel exposed, they may choose to respond in a way that protects their ego rather than show vulnerability. Remember that part of building resilience is tolerating pain, and it is only through accepting any weakness that it can be strengthened.

▌ *There may be internal structures worthy of saving (change does not mean disregarding everything you have done previously) – keep what works.* As personal or organisational growth occurs, becoming the 'new you', or using the 'new way', may result in a desire to reject what may be perceived as the 'old' one. While the behaviour strategies that have worked in the past may no longer be needed so readily, keep them in your archives rather than

remove them as they may be helpful should circumstances
change in future.

▌ *As you start work you may encounter hidden surprises,*
resistance or adaptability. Whatever the response to the
work you are doing, reflect on it. When you ask yourself
'Why did I do that?' you will gain a better understanding
of your approach to life – this will be true of others too.
This alone can help you avoid unhelpful habits or repeat
effective actions.

▌ *Be mindful of how the change affects those in the*
immediate environment – negotiation may be necessary.
Those within a wider circle may notice that changes
are going on. Sometimes they may even reject what you
perceive as positive. The only person you can ever 'control'
is yourself, therefore negotiate and communicate with your
network, but you can only adjust your behaviour, not
theirs . . . something they too need to learn.

▌ *The scaffolding (the professionals, mentors, support*
network) used while the change is happening needs to be
appropriate and effective. Surround yourself with people
who are supportive of your growth, whether this is because
they make you feel comfortable, or they nurture you and
help you develop, or support you. Never confuse loyalty or
obligation with effectiveness.

▌ *Redevelopment is an ongoing process and sometimes*
things will falter. In those times it is helpful to accumulate
positive affirmations, thoughts or actions that are within
easy reach and do not need much planning to implement.
For example, while having a spa day may be something
which relaxes you, it requires planning. If a 3-minute
guided or natural sounds meditation is also helpful and
is accessible on your smartphone, then it is a quick and
simple way to give yourself a boost. This is something
that is worth encouraging your teams, and those you are
working to influence, to consider as well.

▌ *Respect the foundation.* A 'new normal' is often best grown through respect for the old, not simply by demolishing it and trying to forget it. Everything you have been through shows you have survived.

Understanding the process of change can help you navigate it

There are many models of change, but this one by Prochaska *et al.* (2002) is one of my preferred because it is complex enough and active in its approach. In describing the type of behaviour you might see at each stage, it identifies a good starting point for anticipation of or response to the conduct of your teams. I would also propose that you look at the **Contemplation** stage as proactive rather than responsive – you may be making changes without the need for a problem to have manifested, but to prepare for what could be reasonably foreseeable.

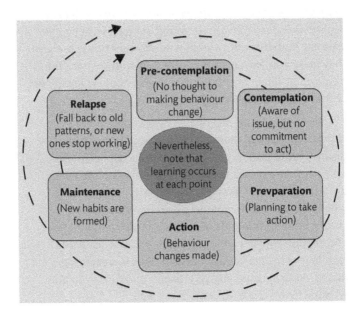

The way you might consider this model in practice is to see yourself currently in the state of **Pre-contemplation**. Everything is ok, but let's say you have identified some areas in which you might wish – at some point – to expand into (perhaps take a sneaky peak back at your response to the SWOT analysis in Chapter 2). You would then be in the **Contemplation** stage – aware that you might like to do something sometime. By the end of this chapter, I hope you might have moved into **Preparation** – making a commitment to take action. The following activities will help you directly with this. If tomorrow you then start to take **Action**, with consistency you will soon be in **Maintenance** with that new behaviour added or modified. There may well be issues along the way (**Relapse** – again, the remainder of this chapter will help), but soon the new way will become standard operating.

So why not make a start![11]

1. Contemplating your next move

In putting this into practice, let's assume your problem area has been defined in Chapter 2 through the SWOT analysis as a potential area of weakness, an area of threat or as a goal you are trying to attain but do not yet have the resources. (You may wish to take a moment to refer to this now.)

Ask yourself

Holding that goal of change in mind:

▌ What resources do I need in order to be able to effect this change?

▌ What are my options in obtaining them?

▌ Where am I, right now, in doing the above?

---

[11]Note that there are more steps in my walkthrough of the model than in the model, but this is because I would like you to be aware of other considerations within each stage.

Don't limit yourself to a habitual approach. Even if it is more common to recruit talent to fill gaps, consider also the options of upskilling, collaborating inter-department or with the wider network, or contracting. The key to your brainstorm is in exploring your options with the goal in mind.

2. Once you have your options – prepare your action

Reflect

Thinking back to the exercises in Chapter 3, did you recognise if you were a 'jump in' type of person, or did you take the time to plan?

Depending on the context, either can be very effective, and there will be times when the ability to do both will serve you well.

When you are looking at a 'non-responsive' change – that is, a change which you are implementing pro-actively – there is time to plan, and a considered approach is likely to bring the greatest rewards. Unfortunately, because it is likely that you will often live life in a fast-paced way when the opportunity to plan presents itself, there is a chance you may not recognise it for what it is.

WHEN YOU HAVE TIME – OPTIMISE IT
TIME IS A PRECIOUS GIFT

I hope that is clear enough.

Action planning

By taking action now, when there is no emergency you can:

State your goal clearly: _____

Identify the steps you need to take	Identify who can help	Reflection and notes

3. Review how the change is going

There is a space for notes in the above table because it is essential that you remain aware of any issues that arose.

It is worth remembering at this point, that while one habitual response to failure is to accept it and let it go, sometimes an extra reflection is helpful. The reason comes down to a sense of being in control. If something goes wrong and you let it go, you may be blindsided should it happen again. If you note it and reflect on it soon after, there is a greater chance you can do so at a time of your choosing – this is very empowering.

Further it is helpful not just to think about the practical outcomes (and issues), but the personal ones as well – if members of the community you are working to support are troubled, reflecting on their responses is important to maintain your relationship and may offer insights into new solutions.

4. Be mindful of the importance of reviewing practically and personally

Reviewing change can draw lessons from the models of both Kolb (1984) and Argyris and Schön (1978).

Kolb's method was simple (single loop):

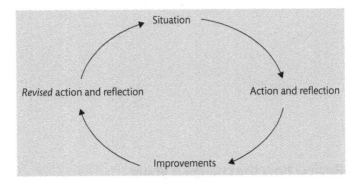

Situation – Action – Results (reflect on them and revise the action).

For Argyris and Schön (double loop) it was important not just to reflect on the action but to challenge the initial assumption, leading in turn to the amended action:

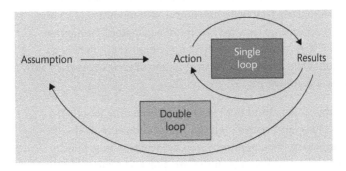

For example: You wish to extend into a new market:

▌ You notice there is competition from niche firms and you do not have the specialist knowledge to be confident in taking that step.

▌ Following consultation where your teams have stated they have no time to take on the niche skill and are happy not to do so, you make the decision to hire two new staff members to take on the niche projects.

▌ On reflection you notice that the motivation of your current team has reduced.

Using 'single loop' you might be tempted simply to stop hiring and change the approach to upskilling your teams, but by exploring the assumption (retuning to the consultation stage rather than the action), you may find out that the team feels overworked and would have benefitted from one staff member being hired to help their workload.

Even in consultation, people may not have fully formulated their thinking. (When under pressure to think, your first answer may not be the most accurate.) It is only when they have had a bit of time (sometimes after the initial solution is implemented) that they are able to unpick their considerations.

By using the 'double loop' and reflecting on the initial assumptions, you may also find solutions for achieving better accuracy in that first, consultation, stage too.

5. Maintain the new methods (and remember to celebrate results)

Change is hard, and one form of motivation is to give updates on success. One of the most historical, successful and common forms of behaviour change is positive reinforcement from Skinner's Operant Learning Theory (Skinner, 1968) where new behaviour is consistently rewarded. Consequently, not only does this process aid the establishment of the new methods, but it is likely to act as a motivator as your teams recognise their efforts have been noticed.

For example: 'We asked, you did'

I am suggesting a variation on the 'you asked, we did' with a focus on gratitude and appreciation that you asked, and your team came through. It also gives you a bit of a boost to reflect on that statement for what that might mean to you as well!

Think about how much more motivated you are when you (and especially when others!) begin to see muscle definition after starting an exercise regime – it is much easier to maintain a new habit when you can either see the results, or someone is reminding you that 'it's working' – ideally both!

Unfortunately, however, a common gripe from teams I train is that 'We work really hard to implement change, and no-one ever tells us how it went.'

Perhaps take a moment to reflect on some past changes to see if you have been clear on acknowledging the positive outcomes to your team as well as the initial need for change.

Try this

Use this table as part of your understanding of how your company has been functioning when it comes to implementing change.

If you are unsure of whether previous success was conveyed, leave it blank. Further, or alternatively, if you are sure success was conveyed, also reflect on how successful your chosen method of communication was – not everyone reads emails nor attends the winter parties when annual reviews may be read out.

Checklist

Reason for change e.g. Saving or making money	Success measure e.g. Profit of £n	How and when was this success conveyed to the team?

If you are satisfied that your teams know that their responses and actions have been key to success, you can always use it as a checklist for implementing future innovations.

6. Regroup (address slip ups, new directions, and troubleshoot on targets)

What do you do when things go wrong? The 'knee jerk' response is common where corrective changes are made and the previous method swept away never to be spoken of again.

At this point, I flag the start of this chapter – *'There may be internal structures worthy of saving, keep what works'*. Not everything, even when it goes wrong, needs to be discarded. When you maintain a mindset of outcomes as 'effective' or 'ineffective' as evaluated by goal attainment, you may notice that while something didn't work in this particular context, it doesn't mean it would not work in a different one.

The same advice applies to leaders implementing change as it does to writers. Even if you no longer wish to use it now, consider keeping it as it may be exactly what you need under different circumstances.

7. Dealing with disruption

While your organisational timeline progresses, so does the larger one of society and changes within the environment may occur which were unexpected. While even the most resilient cannot prepare for every eventuality, it is worthwhile being mindful that organisations exist in the middle of two key circles of constant change:

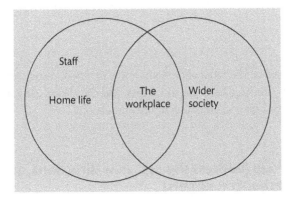

Each timeline runs concurrently, but will have a number of different demands. For example, when you consider home life, while your team may be at the point in their careers where promotion is pending, they may also have pressures at home which may include children and parents (also following their own time paths) for whom they need to care. At the same time, perhaps all businesses are suddenly moving online, or working to reduce their carbon footprint. As an organisation, you need to be flexible, adaptable and have a contingency plan when the need arises. In order for this to happen, you need to be aware of each element of the Venn diagram. Keep your communication open.

8. Live the new way

Once the changes have been made and you are living the 'new normal', spend a moment acknowledging that, while it was tough, it still happened. Again, this is as much for your team's awareness that you recognise them, as for your own in appreciating you met your goals.

I am aware this is the second time I have reminded you to be proud of taking effective action – this is a key part of building resilience. When using Dialectical Behaviour Therapy (DBT), there are three pivotal ways in which clients are encouraged to steel themselves for life's roller coaster:

▌ Accumulate positive experiences (recognise those moments of positivity – the regular practice of gratitude can help with this)

▌ Build mastery (participate in things that you can do, and *recognise when you achieve the things you've had to stretch for*)

▌ Cope ahead (have an idea of your contingency plan for emergencies).

(Course Notes, DBT Diploma, Centre of Excellence, 2018)

Another good reason to recognise mastery is to allow you to make a note (reflectively or physically) of what worked. This may affect the process and is easier next time – or forewarn you against what might cause problems.

9. Optimise what you are doing

Once you are within the day-to-day working of your 'new normal', look at how you might optimise it.

Ask yourself

▌ Are there greater opportunities to involve the community, which in turn could benefit my business?

▌ What contribution am I making on a wider scale – and how do I get people to know that?

One of the common gripes is internal communication, but when it comes to growth, what you say externally is as important.

Conduct a media audit

For example, ask yourself the following:

▌ Is your website conveying your organisation's passion (as well as their identity)?

▌ Are you celebrating what you are doing on your media platforms? This means not only your project and achievements, but consider also promoting your way of working, good wellbeing within your team, innovation and excitement as an organisation. Achievements may attract clients, but working practices bring in – and retain – valuable team players.

▌ Are you utilising the media platforms that upcoming, fresh, potential new clients or team members would use. While

> it's important to have a presence, optimisation is as much about putting the effort in where it will reap the biggest reward. Consider who you wish to attract.

> Is your output consistent with the workplace behaviour within? (Remember – it's important to live your values!)

and throughout: Tread Softly

> *'But I, being poor, have only my dreams;*
> *I have spread my dreams under your feet;*
> *Tread softly because you tread on my dreams.'*
>
> (W. B. Yeats)

I use this poem simply as a reminder of why change is hard – even when it is for the better (and especially when 'it's not broke').

Whether good or bad, places, people – and even procedures – have memories: memories which are often very significant in somebody's personal history. Change is therefore sometimes more than a 'simple alteration' – it can at times represent a huge shift in someone's identity. While often 'change' is made for the better, that is not to say one must disrespect or disregard what has gone before. Even the more challenging recollections have learning and growth embedded.

To quote from an interview I conducted with John Goldwyn, Senior Vice President of WATG London, and the writer of the foreword of this book, 'It is always essential for architects

> Build on what is there – it has memories, values and strengths to have brought you to now

and master planners to take an holistic approach to design. Rather than destroy, our intention is to respect the heritage and preserve the stories of the land, while laying the foundations for more people to thrive.' (Interview with John Goldwyn, *The Chrissy B Show, Sky 191*, 2019).

Building resilience isn't new, it's commemorating and restoring what works and creating room for new growth.

END-OF-CHAPTER TOOLKIT

ADOPT Resilience now

Act

Be seen to be – and actually – challenge and rectify the issues of the past – leave the 'tick box' approach behind once and for all.

> *This week:* Find out – albeit informally – if there is a history of changes, initiatives or restructures where people are unclear of the outcomes. Find out the outcomes! (Even if you discover that some changes did not work out, at least you can learn from them.)

Deal

Ensure changes are understood within the context of learning from history rather than destroying it.

> *This week:* Make a conscious effort to acknowledge the work (and the workers) within your organisation. Don't just focus on achievements, but look also at effort – the personal commitment that has brought about your successes.

Optimise

Despite past issues, ensure there is alignment of values through the 'golden thread' (Sergeant, 2019) approach to communication – everyone, no matter how large the organisation, must be aware of current values and goals. See it as an opportunity to remind people 'you said . . . we did . . .' and thank them!

> *This week:* If you haven't already, highlight a recent change that was implemented; tell your team the results of their efforts.

Prepare

Be prepared – set yourself and your organisation up to respond swiftly as needed, as well as to seize opportunities which may arise. 'Pulse take'. Recognise which trends, directions, or possible opportunities are suitable to your organisation and context. Table a time to discuss potential directions with your senior leaders. Even if you do not implement anything immediately, this awareness means that you are still primed to take action.

> *This week:* Research 'trends in [your sector]' and consider which ones your organisation may benefit from should you choose to explore them further.

Thrive

Seek opportunities to promote and celebrate what you are doing within your wider community.

> *This week:* If you do not already have an active social media platform, create one. Identify your network who can help with publicising your activities, e.g. local newspapers or trade journals. Remember that often the most engaging stories are not simply about the outcome, but the human efforts that went into achieving them. Be proud of your team as well as their results.

Notes

What I did	Date

Reflection (at a later date)

How have my thoughts changed now?

References

Argyris, C. and Schön, D. (1978) *Organizational Learning: A theory of action perspective*. Addison Wesley.

Centre of Excellence (2018) *Dialectical Behaviour Therapy Diploma*. Course Notes.

OECD (2020) *Resilient Cities* https://www.oecd.org/regional/resilient-cities.htm (accessed May 2020).

Kolb, D. A. (1984) *Experiential Learning: Experience as the source of learning and development*. Prentice-Hall.

Prochaska, J. O., Redding, C. A. and Evers, K. E. (2002) The transtheoretical model and stages of change. In A. Glanz, K. Glanz, B. K. Rimer and F. M. Lewis (eds) *Health Behavior and Health Education: Theory, research, and practice* (3rd edn). Jossey-Bass, Inc.

Sergeant, M. (2019) *PR for Humans: How business leaders tell powerful stories*. Practical Inspiration Publishing.

Skinner, B. F. (1968) *The Technology of Teaching*. Meredith Corporation.

Tang, A. (2019) Interview with John Goldwyn, WATG, *The Chrissy B Show, Sky 191*, UCKG.

Yeats, W. B. (c1899) *Aedh Wishes for the Cloths of Heaven* https://www.oneirishrover.com/poem-yeats-wishes-cloths-heaven/ (accessed May 2020).

Be sustainable

'The world is waking up. And change is coming,
whether you like it or not.'

(Greta Thunberg addressing the UN Climate
Action Summit, 2019)

Can you afford not to be sustainable?

While some crises may take us by surprise, we have
known about climate change for some time, but
do you do enough about it? . . . and why should
you care?

Ask yourself

▌ If you had known a crisis you have experienced would
happen – what would you have done about it?

If you would have tried to do something, then it is time to
amp up corporate social responsibility. After all, there is no
point helming a thriving business, if it has no environment to
thrive within.

Reflect

▌ How much unnecessary waste do you produce annually?

▌ How much money could you save if you were more mindful of what to print, to throw, to keep, to replace or restore?

Sustainability and resilience

Sustainability means looking after your organisational resources, reducing waste and building efficiency – this applies to the practices of the micro (business) environment as well as the macro (social) one. It is also essential for your organisation's wider environment to be healthy – as well as its internal one. Further, sustainability is one area which engages community, country and, indeed, world-wide interest and organisations that include it in their agenda are appreciated. *To be resilient, it is important to consider how to maintain and replenish the resources which contribute to survival long term, within your organisation and within the community in which it will thrive.*

Resilient thinking is looking beyond the present. It sees a future that can exist beyond your lifetime. If you want your business, your work – your legacy – to continue beyond you, then you have to look beyond your back yard. There is no point having a business with no community left to engage in it. Therefore sustainability – which affects organisations on the broader scale – must be considered within a book on resilience. It also offers another potential framework through which leaders can promote resilient behaviour. Being sustainable is about maintaining the macro environment within which your organisation will sit. If that disappears, so too does your business. It is no longer someone else's responsibility to deal with: we can all do our bit . . . and if we do – if we *all* work towards that common goal of preserving the world in which we want to thrive –how much more effective will we be?

> **Reflect**
>
> What does 'sustainability' mean to you?
>
> ▌ Not being wasteful?
>
> ▌ Being careful about resources?
>
> ▌ Being able to survive long term?
>
> ▌ Efficiency?

Sustainable practice at both the micro and macro levels can be a major contributor to that ability to survive – and it's a surprisingly simple one to implement. Doing both is also attractive to teams, clients and customers.

You Matter (Wahl, 2020) outlines the three pillars of sustainability as:

▌ Economy

▌ Society

▌ Environment

. . . stated informally as 'profit, people and planet'. A resilient business needs to maintain profit, and the people to generate that success, but awareness of the environment is also essential because no matter how healthy a business is, it can only last as long as the environment within which it is based.

That alone is good reason to be mindful of preserving the environment, but a 'green' outlook in itself also attracts 'people' and 'profit'. As Greta Thunberg said in her 2019 UN Climate Action address, '. . . young people are starting to understand . . . The eyes of all future generations are upon you.'

Seventy-three percent of Millennials will pay more for green products, which demonstrates a commitment towards sustainability (Nielsen, 2015). Girlguiding UK overhauled their badges with a new 2019 programme which includes Upcycling, STEM and politics in order to 'reflect the diversity of girls and modern life in the

21st Century' (Girlguiding UK, 2020). Academic research
has demonstrated that sustainability can also yield
huge financial advantages. Businesses who demonstrate
environmentally sustainable behaviours such as reduced
waste, clean living and 'green' business practices generate a
positive public response when it comes to recruitment and
retention (Lorette, **smallbusiness.chron.com**, 2020).

Patagonia, a profit-based company has seen '. . . its
revenue and profit quadruple' through its position as an
'activist corporation' known also for suing '. . . the Trump
administration in December 2017. President Trump had
announced his plans to reduce the size of two National
Monuments, the Bear Ears red rock canyon and the Grand-
Staircase Escalante. Having been involved with Bear Ears
previously, Patagonia mobilised their legal team to take
protective action filing a motion which named the president
as one of the defendants. Thus, Blakely (2018) concluded,
'. . . Consumer and employers are looking for deeper purpose
from companies.' However, this is not greenwashing – the
company genuinely cares about making a difference. Part of
their mission statement reads: 'We know that our business
activity . . . is part of the problem. We work steadily to
change our business practices . . . seek not only to do less
harm but more good.' (Patagonia Core Values, 2020).

Current societal trends recognise 'green' organisations are
a draw for the ever-more eco-friendly workforce (Atikunde,
2015) as well as increases in customer spend. However, with
Nielsen's 2015 survey of 30,000 consumers in 60 countries
showing 66% of consumers are willing to pay higher prices
for environmentally sustainable products, I must add a word
of warning against 'greenwashing' (Watson, 2016). Patagonia
is sincere, others trying to capitalise on faux purpose are
often found out.

However, being 'green' is *not* just about personal profit.

Sustainability is in everybody's interest when it comes to
resilience because it ultimately promotes survival of the

species . . . although, as with many things that are in the 'public interest', the public is not always interested.

A recent paper on Global Health Research concluded that shared or 'Open Access' publications build global research capacity, and '. . . limiting public access can negatively impact implementation and outcomes of health policy' (Smith *et al.*, 2017). In medical crises, sharing of research data was immediate to have the greatest opportunity to establish a cure. Yet, cancer or diabetes drugs are still being sold for a huge profit with '. . . most patients getting second rate treatment' because 'Physicians are not good at challenging payers' (Packer, **medpagetoday.com**, 2018).

Selfishness can prevent societal benefit.

Research from the University of Geneva found that individuals who show more self-focused 'egotistical' brain mapping are less concerned about future consequences (which will not 'definitely' affect them); they care more about short-term outcomes, in comparison to individuals who show more 'altruistic' brain activity and treat long-term and short-term consequences with a similar concern (Brosch *et al.*, 2018). However, Brosch and his team noted that '. . . the solution to many of mankind's current problems . . . is based on the *need to overcome selfish impulses* . . .' and thus recommended that psychologists and other professionals seek to find ways of improving societal concern.

Notably though, selfishness is being called out: The concept of greenwashing

The term 'greenwashing' was first used in the mid-eighties to encapsulate behaviour where companies presented a show of '. . . sustainability claims to cover a questionable environmental record' (Watson, 2016). Rather than making sincere efforts, some brands merely capitalised on the power of seeming 'environmentally friendly'. The definition of 'greenwashing' has also extended to include businesses that spend more on appearing green than actually living by their advertising.

However, public awareness is growing along with their interest in organisations with a 'purpose'. Many companies have come under scrutiny for making false or exaggerated environmentally friendly claims including Nestlé, Charmin and car companies such as Mercedes-Benz (Truth in Advertising, 2019), and environmentally-driven PR crises such as the BP Gulf of Mexico Oil Spill in 2010 (Shogren, 2011); and Volkswagen's 'diesel dupe' (Hotten, 2015) can take a lot more effort to recover from.

People are growing wise to diversion tactics; the regulators across the world are getting more astute in their investigations; and, if found out, deceptive labelling and advertising potentially yield high fines as well as public embarrassment (American Bar Association, 2019). The rise of 'cancel culture', especially within social media, may also see such behaviours, along with greenwashing, leading to boycotting of previously popular brands.

You cannot be expected to overhaul everything, but perhaps you can make little changes or offset what you take from natural resources by putting something else back in.

It's easy being green – so why not be sincere in your efforts?

Find out

▌ What does my organisation currently do to promote sustainability?

- E.g. incentives to 'leave the car at home'
- Recycling facilities or providing reusable flasks and mugs
- Collaborations with ethical suppliers
- Turning off lights/electronics/heating as appropriate

➤

- Sustainable products

- Being a paperless office

- Keeping the thermostat low (bring a blanket!)

- Keeping desk plants

- Recycling electronics

- Holding virtual meetings rather than travelling

▌ Are my teams aware of these practices? (Can you provide training if not?)

Reflect

Think about the resources you use every day within your business.

▌ What simple practices do I engage in to make a small, simple, but positive contribution to the environment? For example, recycling, going paperless?

Try this

Ask your teams the same question and encourage them to share.

Even encourage a training event which only uses recyclable materials.

Ask yourself

▌ What little changes could I make to my daily practices? For example, bringing in a refillable flask rather than buying cups.

▌ Which of these can I implement easily within my team?

It's not necessarily about being the global leader, or creating a green revolution (not yet anyway), but it's possible to do your bit.

Further, when it comes to sustainability, bear in mind environmental resources are not the only ones needing protection.

Remember the human of 'human resources' too

Doing 'your' bit relies on motivating the 'you' within the 'your'. Therefore it is as important to sustain 'people', the human resource which can erode as easily as the environment if overlooked.

In a recent training session on managing a budget, I tasked teams to save money in three sites. Here is an abridged version:

What might you do?

You are a strategy group with three sites for your organisation.

Two (South and East) are leased and coming up for renewal. They are located at the North, South and East of a town about the size of Northampton (population approx. 250,000 and around 80.77 square km with a good bus system). Each serves the local community.

The one in the North is near the university and is thriving, the one in the South is sustaining itself. The one in the East is losing money.

The one in the North is fast becoming the flagship, the one in the East spends more time fielding complaints of poor service.

You want to save money to bid for a new contract near your North site. What might you do?

This is a hugely simplified example of the case presented – and more details were given to delegates on request, but it was the thought process and ensuing behaviours that were the most notable.

The morning session of this particular training focused on the importance of working for leadership that was aware that people were more than 'capital' or 'resources'. Teams have their own lives, commitments and at times their own storms to ride. The morning session always concludes with delegates acknowledging the importance of looking behind the role to recognise the person behind it.

In their afternoon role there were many inspiring ideas to promote the North site, to grow the flagship and make an impact within the field as a market leader. But I also noted the following phrases:

- 'Well just close down the East site'
- 'We can move everyone to the North or South'
- 'If they're struggling then they can be helped when they move across'

. . . it was as simple as moving little pins on a seating plan – and ultimately the organisation would benefit.

These were the same delegates who had complained about how some of their own managers seemed oblivious to their concerns, how they were going through the third restructure in 5 years, how they struggled getting to work because of previous relocation.

Your commitment to the human resource needs to be an *ongoing, active and sincere one*. Like 'greenwashing', good employees will vote with their feet if they find that businesses do not live up to their values. '. . . there are three elements to a culture: behaviours, systems and practices, all guided by an overarching set of values. A great culture is . . . when all three . . . are aligned and line up with the organisation's espoused values. When gaps start to appear . . . great employees leave' (Daimler, 2018).

It's also very easy to overlook the elements that *help* you reach your goal when you are excited about achieving one.

People use their free will. As much as they may pursue loyalty or wish to be amenable, if they cannot see the fruits of their labour, they will leave. This makes them as valuable an asset to actively sustain as wildlife and the environment.

The 'funding committee exercise' is just a simple thought experiment. Hopefully through making you (and the teams that did the exercise and reflected on their thinking) more aware of the ease at which one can become blindsided by goal chasing, it will remind you to stop and think about *who* will help get you there, *as part of* the *how.* It will be people who will help you effect change, so make sure you are sustaining them too!

Sustainable practices is a win-win for human emotional resilience

If you are sustaining, you are surviving. If you have survived, you can bounce back. If you can bounce, you can thrive. Sustainability – whether through preserving human resources or environmental ones (ideally both) contributes to businesses standing firm.

What is even more of a bonus is that some environmentally sustainable practices have a huge positive impact on the wellbeing of your human resources!

Benefitting the planet can benefit people: Green workplaces can improve health

In 2018 Singapore launched the 'Green Mark for Healthier Workplaces'. The five features they outlined for a sustainable workplace benefitting both people and planet were:

1. Sustainable design and management (of the basic building design)

2. Energy and response management (e.g. water, electricity, heating, air conditioning)

3. The office environment (e.g. lighting, glare control, overall comfort)

4. Workplace health and wellbeing (e.g. food options, fitness programmes, smoking cessation programmes, biophilic properties)

5. Advanced features (e.g. energy monitoring, energy disclosure, workplace health promotion)

(BCA Green Mark, 2018)

Find out

- Is your organisation making improvements in any of the above five areas?
- Do your teams know about this – and if not, how can you communicate it?
- What more could you do? (Consider raising this at your next team or leadership meeting.)

Environmental psychologists will agree that behaviour can be shaped by the setting. Having areas that generate a sense of wellbeing such as designs capturing our biophilic preference for curves, or buildings constructed from natural materials such as wood, the smell of pine or evergreens or the sound of running water can all contribute to energising your human resource. Conversely, certain contexts are conducive to crime, e.g. the 'Broken Windows' theory (Kelling and Wilson, 1982) or that population density leads to aggression as dramatised in Ballard's 2012 *High-Rise*, based on Calhoun's 1960s 'Rat utopia' – where over-crowded work spaces, no opportunity for privacy, a lack of consistent personal territory can be as problematic for your teams as constant demands or uncontained client stress. Creating a positive environment through sustainable practices is an easy win, and will help the planet, your people and, in turn, most likely your profits.

As well as *improvements* to wellbeing you can *protect* what you have

In the same way as the idea 'you can make money or you can save money', the same is true of human energy. As well as making little changes that may contribute to *improving* the mental and emotional wellbeing of your teams, also consider how you can *protect* them from burnout while in a changing environment.

Consider these three conservational ways of looking after who you have:

1. *Make sure your expectations align with your teams:* According to a 2019 Gallup poll, only 60% of the American teams asked knew what was expected of them at work. Ambiguity and uncertainly can lead to stress – even in a customer service interaction you only need to reflect on how you feel when you don't know what is going on compared to when you are aware of the possible outcomes.

   – **Do you** know what your organisational goals are?

   – **Can you** ensure they are communicated to your team?

   – **Are you** mindful that each individual also knows what is expected of them within their role (the appraisal is a good time to check alignment, as well as ask what your team's personal aspirations are)?

2. *Do you know if your team are able to 'switch off' outside work? (Are you?):* Because of the ease of connection, and the global nature of most workplaces, it is not uncommon to be managing work issues within personal time. Encourage your team to 'switch off' outside the working hours, and try to model this behaviour yourself.

- Be aware of team members who may be using work as a reason to escape from personal difficulties. What options for support do you offer in these instances?

3. *Consider adding wellbeing workshops to your team's training schedule:* Rather than the soft skills of team building, consider offering training which reminds your teams to look after themselves[12] – this does not mean a 'mindfulness workshop', but perhaps collaborating with wellbeing and self-development professionals who can support personal growth; or offering your team group or individual coaching.

Remember energy, in *all* its forms, is a valuable and finite resource

You cannot do 'everything', but you can do something – and something is ok.

When you are working to make changes and implement the inspirational ideas you have, or support your team's wellbeing and perhaps in turn productivity and certainly longevity, remember that energy (animal, mineral or vegetable) is a finite resource, and it needs to be recharged before burnout.

Ask yourself

▌ How am I best energised? (e.g. With people I love? Alone? Engaged in a hobby?)

▌ How often do I do this?

▌ How can I make more time for it?

---

[12] At the time of writing I have noticed that I am being required to speak more on wellbeing in addition to my current leadership development programmes. Such training includes work on self-value and empowerment (similar to the themes in Part 1 of this book) in order to build the individual from within, giving their personal growth a stronger root.

A quick word here about introversion and extraversion.
These terms are colloquially understood as 'extraverts are
outgoing and introverts are quiet loners'. As alluded to in the
'Optimise' section of the Introduction to this book, this – albeit
common – understanding is an oversimplification of Carl
Jung's original 1921 approach. According to Jung these two
concepts are *attitudes* – 'Each person seems to be energised
more by the external world (extraversion) or the internal world
(introversion)'. They are preferences. An extravert can perform
well in a quiet setting, and the introvert vice versa, but they are
best *energised* by settings relating to their preference.

In modern usage, the term altered to suggest that the
extravert is happiest in a social setting and the introvert in
a more solitary one, and contemporary usage includes the
term 'ambivert' to denote someone who may enjoy specific
group company and specific quiet pursuits. However, Jung's
approach is deeper than contemporary usage – i.e. it is a
logical leap to presume that someone who draws energy from
social settings will perform well within them, but it is the
*drawing (*or *replenishing) of energy that is key to wellbeing*
and *building resilience*. This is how I would like you to
consider your preference.

Leadership can deplete your own energy reserves, and the
accomplished leader, regardless of preference will be able to
perform in a variety of settings. If you are aware of how (and
with whom) you are *best energised*, spending more time in
that context is likely to give you that boost you need when
you most require it.

Also ask yourself

▌ With whom – or when doing what – do I feel most degraded?
... and if you can, try to avoid that or limit exposure.

The human resource is as important to sustain as the natural
world is.

Be aware of other means of erosion to your sustainability

The following may be areas in which your good work can be corroded if unchecked:

- **Societal trends:** 'Greenwashing' has already been addressed in this chapter – but do not allow a drive for profit to undermine sincerity. Consumer and client behaviour changes and can be highly influential, but always try to keep abreast of the full story. Gluten free foods, for example, are a very welcomed addition to the supermarket aisles for coeliac sufferers as well as those with food intolerances, but they are not necessarily a 'trend'. Such a diet is not healthy for everyone, so while a trend for smart devices may have led to charging stations in most cafés, the creation of solely gluten-free restaurants may not necessarily be as shrewd an investment. Before implementing modifications, be aware of what you are doing, why and the wider consequences.

- **Laws and regulations:** Make sure all practices and communications meet legal responsibilities. Don't become the next '#fakenews' story. Xenon Group identify key UK sustainability regulations:

    The Environmental Protection Act 1990
    This covers Integrated Pollution Control; Waste; Statutory Nuisance and Clean Air.

    The Environment Act 1995
    This act founded the UK Government Environmental Agency, and focuses on Air and Water Quality, Contaminated Land and Waste.

    The Waste Electrical and Electronic Equipment (WEEE) Directive 2007 and *The Directive on the Restriction of the use of certain Hazardous Substances (RoHS)* in electrical and electronic equipment *2003*.

These focus on the requirements and standards for household appliances, IT and telecoms, consumer and lighting equipment, electrical tools, toys, leisure and sport equipment and medical devices with the WEEE also requiring appropriate disposal and treatment of used equipment. *The Environmental Permitting Regulations 2010* and *The Waste Framework Directive 2008* also set out procedures for the disposal of waste and hazardous waste to avoid endangering health.

The Climate Change Act 2008
A groundbreaking act making the UK the '. . . first country in the world to have a legally binding long-term framework to cut carbon emissions'. It also introduced a system of 'carbon budgets' where if emissions rise in one sector, the UK has to achieve a corresponding fall in another.

(Xenon Group, 2018)

Indeed, the UK is proud of mobilising to make a positive contribution to the environment. Ultimately, the world is a shared space, and sometimes collaboration towards a mutually beneficial goal yields better long-term results than competition and scarcity.

Your commitment to the 'good' can have positive consequences for the 'greater good'

Kirkland (2019) suggests that there are three things that need to occur which motivate even the most selfish to address wider societal issues:

▍ Awareness

▍ Responsibility

▍ Action.

In other words:

- Awareness that you are in some way a part of the problem
- Knowledge of options to fix it
- Said options being easy to implement, or at the very least not detrimental to the perceived comfort of the person taking action.

Then:

- Apply the principles of 'encouraging greater good' behaviour: Know you are part of the cause of the issue; Know that a 'fix' (especially a small one) is possible; Know that your 'fix' is easy (and not detrimental to you).

Think about it

- Throughout this book so far you have been made aware that resilience is about survival
- You have been given a number of methods to improve your chances in a challenging world
- They are all simple to implement.

Sustainable practice is an easy, and essential, contribution towards your own resilience.

You benefit your own survival, your people, your profits and, while doing so, the environment at large.

END-OF-CHAPTER TOOLKIT

ADOPT Resilience now

Act

Be conscious of how hard your human resources are working and help them preserve or replenish their energy.

This week: Ask your team how they are best energised and consider how you can incorporate that into your daily practice – e.g. if your team comprises many introverts in an open-plan office, consider whether you can change the set up of the room, or provide 'quiet areas' – or even if extraverts may benefit from screens to protect from distraction, but a more bustling communal area for taking breaks. People also thrive when they have their own space (University of Queensland, 2019), so consider ensuring they all have areas they can personalise.

Deal

Be aware of the effect of the environment on wellbeing and ensure spaces are conducive to productivity.

This week: Observe your working environment, are there changes you can make which merge environmental as well as societal (people) sustainability. For example, a policy to reduce waste where results in terms of profit are fed back; encouraging people to keep plants in their working area if possible; or team days where you contribute to local community areas.

Optimise

While remaining sincere, communicate the positive work you are doing through social media or trade journals.

This week: Identify any promotional opportunities including creating a hashtag for social media.

Prepare

Ensure you are prepared for sustainability changes on a global scale.

This week: Familiarise yourself with the sustainability directives and regulations that may affect your business and begin to lay the groundwork to incorporate them.

Thrive

Seek ways of encouraging your teams to recognise the benefits of collaborative sustainability. Rather than approach it as something *'we all have to do'*, acknowledge it as something that advantages your own wellbeing and lifestyle.

This week: Recognise your personal benefits of sustainable practice. For example, how much do you enjoy fresh air when you run? If relevant, consider how your children will benefit. Has your fitness improved by opting for walking instead of driving your car?

Notes

What I did	Date

Reflection (at a later date)

How have my thoughts changed now?

References

American Bar Association (2019) Greenwashing: What your clients should avoid, *ABA* https://www.americanbar.org/groups/gpsolo/publications/gp_solo/2011/september/greenwashing_what_your_clients_should_avoid/ (accessed May 2020).

Atikunde, A. (2015) Why being a green business has become more attractive to small-business owners, *American Express* https://www.americanexpress.com/en-us/business/trends-and-insights/articles/why-being-a-green-business-has-become-more-attractive-to-small-business-owners/ (accessed May 2020).

Ballard, J. G. (2012) *High-Rise*. Liveright.

BCA Green Mark (2018) https://www.bca.gov.sg/GreenMark/others/GM_HW_2018_Pilot.pdf (accessed May 2020).

Blakely, L. (2018) Patagonia's unapologetically political strategy and the massive business it has built, *Inc.* https://www.inc.com/lindsay-blakely/patagonia-2018-company-of-the-year-nominee.html (accessed May 2020).

Brosch, T., Stussi, Y., Desrichard, O. and Sander, D. (2018) Not my future? Core values and the neural representation of future events. *Cognitive, Affective & Behavioral Neuroscience,* Vol. 18, 476–484 https://doi.org/10.3758/s13415-018-0581-9

Calhoun, J. B. (1962) Population density and social pathology. *Scientific American*, Vol. 206, No. 2, 139-148.

Daimler, M. (2018) Why great employees leave 'great cultures', *Harvard Business Review* https://hbr.org/2018/05/why-great-employees-leave-great-cultures (accessed May 2020).

Gallup poll cited in Stratton, M. (2019) How to protect your team from burnout, *Thrive Global* https://thriveglobal.com/stories/protect-team-burnout-stress-managing-tips/ (accessed May 2020).

Girlguiding UK (2020) https://www.girlguiding.org.uk/ (accessed May 2020).

Hotten, R. (2015) Volkswagen: The scandal explained https://www.bbc.co.uk/news/business-34324772 (accessed May 2020).

Jung, C. G. (1921) *Psychologische Typen*, Rascher Verlag, Zurich – translation H. G. Baynes, 1923.

Kelling, G. L. and Wilson, J. Q. (1982) Broken Windows: The police and neighborhood safety. *The Atlantic* https://www.theatlantic.com/magazine/archive/1982/03/broken-windows/304465/ (accessed June 2019).

Kirkland, G. (2019) How to successfully motivate people to care about the earth, *Environment* https://www.environment.co.za/environmental-issues/how-to-successfully-motivate-people-to-care-about-the-earth.html (accessed November 2019).

Lorette, K. (2020) Why businesses should go green, *Chron*, https://smallbusiness.chron.com/businesses-should-green-766.html (accessed May 2020).

Nielsen poll (2015) cited in Curtin, M. (2018) 73 percent of Millennials are willing to spend more money on this 1 type of product, *Inc.* https://www.inc.com/melanie-curtin/73-percent-of-millennials-are-willing-to-spend-more-money-on-this-1-type-of-product.html (accessed May 2020).

Packer, M. (2018) It's official! Curing patients is bad for business, *MedPage Today* https://www.medpagetoday.com/blogs/revolutionandrevelation/72407 (accessed May 2020).

Patagonia Core Values (2020) https://www.patagonia.com/company-info.html (accessed May 2020).

Shogren, E. (2011) BP: A textbook example of how not to handle PR, *NPR* https://www.npr.org/2011/04/21/135575238/bp-a-textbook-example-of-how-not-to-handle-pr?t=1581422323487 (accessed May 2020).

Smith, E. *et al.* (2017) Knowledge sharing in global health research – the impact, uptake and cost of open access to scholarly literature. *Health Research Policy and Systems,* Vol. 15, 73 https://doi.org/10.1186/s12961-017-0235-3

Thunberg, G. (2019) UN Climate Action Summit https://www.npr.org/2019/09/23/763452863/transcript-greta-thunbergs-speech-at-the-u-n-climate-action-summit (accessed May 2020).

Truth in Advertising, Inc. (2019) Earth Day 2020: 6 Companies Accused of Greenwashing https://www.truthinadvertising.org/six-companies-accused-greenwashing/ (accessed September 2020).

University of Queensland (2019) *Anthropology of Current World Issues*, University of Queensland lectures, March 2019.

Wahl, D. C. (2020) Sustainability – What is it? Definition, principles and examples, *You Matter* https://youmatter.world/en/definition/definitions-sustainability-definition-examples-principles/ (accessed May 2020).

Watson, B. (2016) The troubling evolution of corporate greenwashing. *The Guardian* https://www.theguardian.com/sustainable-business/2016/aug/20/greenwashing-environmentalism-lies-companies (accessed May 2020).

Xenon Group (2018) 7 Key Pieces of Sustainability Related Legislation that you Should be Aware of https://www.xenongroup.co.uk/knowledge-centre/csr-and-sustainability/6-key-pieces-of-sustainability-related-legislation-that-you-should-be-aware-of (accessed September 2020).

Resilience in practice

9

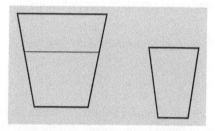

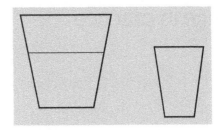

You have one *15-litre* jug filled up to *11 litres*

You have one empty *9-litre* jug

Puzzle 2: How do you measure exactly 2 litres?

Puzzle 3: How do you measure exactly 5 litres?

Puzzle 4: How do you measure exactly 14 litres?

Mathematicians among you, or those who have come across this problem before will know that the first problem is impossible, but the next three are solvable. However if you tried and were unsuccessful you may have decided *not* to try at the second puzzle.

You would also not be alone.

Beaton (2016) in an article for *Forbes*, gives three examples of failure breeding failure – failure on a task may result in you being hindered by mistakes rather than motivating you to learn from them; failures can impede your ability to concentrate; and if you are simply *told* you have failed, your next task may be negatively affected. Indeed those who have been on a diet and fallen off the waggon may know how easy it is to throw in the towel that day.

Therefore, this chapter focuses on *living* the organisational values which will help you bounce back so it won't be a case of 'you never know your strength until you are tested' but rather, living daily in such a way that you and your team know, even if the worst happens, you'll survive.

If you practise resilient behaviours every day they become natural to you when you need to use them to rebuild.

> The best time to build resilience is before the point of crisis

Ask yourself

Think back to Chapter 8 and ask yourself:

What IF you were the organisation caught greenwashing?

What IF you had to face an internal scandal?

What IF you had to rebuild yourself from the ground up?

Resilience is about 'knowing' you will be ok

Ask yourself

When things are tough what do you say to yourself?

Often the responses are similar to the original survival instinct 'fight', 'flight', freeze':

'Fighters' may roll their sleeves up and get on with it.

Those in 'Flight' may go into hiding.

Those who 'Freeze' may choose to 'wait it out' until the position gets a little clearer.

There is no ultimate 'right or wrong' way to approach a challenge, and often a combination of the above will be most successful.

Those who run in with a solution may (if the circumstances are not time dependent) do well to keep their head down, or to wait before taking action as their response may be more astute and measured with time; those who hide or wait will at some point need to take action.

This chapter will therefore offer five easy practices to develop your organisational resilience so that you know if things go wrong – you *will* be ok:

1. Building trust
2. Own and *live* your narrative
3. Responding to errors
4. Flexibility (the ability to change direction)
5. Engaging with your community (notable through electronic word of mouth)

Building trust within your teams (*as well as* through customer loyalty)

The Organisational Resilience Index

The BSI Group developed a 16-point awareness audit in 2017, identifying the areas organisations needed to invest in for greatest survival potential. They fell within four key categories.

- **Leadership**: including visibility of the senior team and their work to establish high-quality finance, resource and reputational risk management.
- **People**: awareness of and engagement with the organisational culture as well as the level of trust in the organisations.
- **Procedures**: the level and quality of accountability, health and safety, network and overall governance.

▌**Customer/Client need**: customer or client need as it falls within governance, but also with a view to the future. This includes the ability to adapt to changes in demand as well as to innovate.

In short, within a resilient organisation, your people need to trust you to lead and you need to trust them to follow. Trust begins firstly with your own people because they will be the people who will perform to generate the loyalty of clients and customers!

Try a 'trust audit'

There are many ways you can measure the trust within your organisation without foisting psychometrics; however, you need to be clear on the following:

1. WHAT are you looking for?

Tucker (2006) proposed that trust could fall within one of three areas:

- Short-term trust measurable through rankings such as targets being met or positive feedback on products. This demonstrates that your team are performing well, but it doesn't reveal much about loyalty long term.

- Medium-term trust. Tucker also calls this 'reflexive mistrust' and defines it as the idea that there needs to be a level of trust in order for the company to function and suggests it is best measured with a survey such as the 'Grunig relationship instrument', which measures the dimensions of competence, integrity and dependability.

- Long-term trust demonstrated by loyalty (customers/ clients and your own people) as well as the '. . . level of forgiveness in a crisis' (Tucker, 2006).

➤

2. WHAT are you comparing to?

If you are looking at short-term trust, are you comparing performance now and perhaps to 5 or 10 years ago?

Are you comparing performance now with projected performance?

Similarly long-term trust could be examined by looking at a previous crisis and comparing your company's performance with a similar organisation.

3. WHAT are you measuring?

You may choose to measure any of the following:

- Performance
- Sales targets
- Retention
- Recruitment
- Customer or client loyalty
- Reduction in legal feels
- Media reports
- Employee satisfaction scores
- Employee turnover

. . . or other areas you feel would best inform your practice.

4. HOW will you respond to the results?

The information that you gather will enable you to identify patterns of behaviour, which in turn may give you an insight into how your teams responded to certain situations. It will enable you to highlight times and conduct focus groups to gain more insights into the beliefs of your team.

5. Also DECIDE if you are going to involve your team in the audit, and if so, explain its purpose and how you intend to proceed. Then of course, share the results, actions and outcomes and decide if you will do a follow-up data review.

A trust audit, although time consuming, is another way to open dialogue between yourself and your team, as well as gain insight into how they perceive your organisation. This can in turn give you a starting point with regards to making any changes or improvements, as well as offer information as to what motivates (or damages) much-needed loyalty.

Loyalty is key in times of trouble

While many businesses focus on loyalty from clients and customers, loyalty from your team means that they will often work harder (improving said loyalty from clients and customers), but they may also stay longer – so you benefit from their skills as they develop them (Suttie, 2017). Further, they can be valuable allies when things go wrong.

Years of psychological research have continually demonstrated that social support is an essential factor in times of difficulty. More recently findings have gone on to show that social support causes physiological changes in the brain, which helps inhibit the stress response (e.g. Ozbay *et al.*, 2007). Anecdotally too, it is most common for stories of resilience to include someone or something the protagonist can believe in, despite feeling that the rest of the world is against them. (This can, in times of loneliness, be faith as well as a person.)

It is notable, however, that loyalty cannot be blind and it is important, when things are less emotional in the aftermath of a crisis, to take time to reflect on mistakes to learn where your behaviours could change in future; but having someone to trust certainly helps bolster your ability to cope (Suttie, 2017).

Own and *live* your narrative

▌ Are you aware of how your organisation is perceived within your community? What about within the field?

▌ What messages are you consistently putting out (do you regularly review your social media, your websites, advertising materials and any customer-facing touchpoints)?

▌ How does your day-to-day behaviour reflect the mission statement of company values that you present?

Ask your team to describe what they believe the values of your organisation to be.

Ask them if they know what the current company values are.

If there is a lack of alignment, ask your team to suggest how to better connect day-to-day behaviours with company values (it may mean changing one or both!).

Your story is important, no matter what the heritage, and especially if it can show growth.

It was announced in 2019 that Monica Lewinsky was a producer on the *American Crime Story* dramatisation of the 'Bill Clinton Sex Scandal' (Edelstein, 2019). In taking the power of the narrative that for many years had shaped perceptions of her, she was refusing to be controlled by the shame. She expressed her personal growth in her TED Talk *The Price of Shame* in 2015: at that time, her voice began to be recognised – so was her intelligence, ability and all the other positive personal traits lost in the media circus of not having 'sexual relations with that woman', which plagued Lewinsky for almost 20 years.

Lewinsky, as she said in her TED Talk, 'made a mistake', but for 17 years she was shamed and publicly humiliated for it. With the advent of the internet she was '. . . judged by many and known by few'. The social media fallout was not necessarily to present the truth, but rather, again according to her to '. . . get clicks and sell papers', and it only gets worse. Electronic word of mouth (EWoM) is hugely effective whether personally and professionally for engaging the world to positive or negative ends.

Don't wait until a mistake takes your voice out of your hands – make sure the narrative that you are expressing is exactly what you want it to be – and that you then live up to it.

Responding to errors

If people sense you are not being honest, they will often make it their mission to pursue you until they feel vindicated.

Own up: People *do* make mistakes, after all we are only human. The most effective thing to do is to take responsibility and learn what went wrong to avoid the same situation in the future. Trying to cover up often leads to a loss of respect.

Take responsibility: Taking responsibility is not about apportioning 'blame'. Blame is simply 'finger pointing' and deflection, whereas when you take responsibility and ownership – you have power over that contribution (however big or small). Don't see it as 'accepting blame' but rather 'taking power'.

Accepting responsibility following a partnership or merger can be a powerful way of generating trust in your ethics from clients and teams alike. When Diageo took on Distillers, the UK distributor of the thalidomide drug, they earmarked over £150m to be given to survivors over three decades (Thalidomide UK, 2005). Even though something may not have been your fault – if it has become your problem, you need to deal with it.

Learn from it: Sometimes your choice is whether to follow one mistake with another. Do not let the 'sunk-cost fallacy' (Arkes and Blumer, 1985) sink you. Just because you have already made an investment you regret, such as ordering too much food, do not give yourself indigestion trying to eat it to get your money's worth.

When something has gone wrong, try using the 'Five Whys Technique' developed by Toyota (Serrat, 2009), which involves asking the question 'why' five times, in order to get to the root cause.

This is an example from Spear (2009):

A vehicle will not start.

1. *Why?* – The battery is dead.
2. *Why?* – The alternator is not functioning.
3. *Why?* – The alternator belt has broken.
4. *Why?* – The alternator belt was well beyond its useful service life and not replaced.
5. *Why?* – The vehicle was not maintained according to the recommended service schedule.

This fifth answer enables you to take action, e.g. check how regularly the service schedule is adhered to; assess the effectiveness of those conducting the service; examine the regularity of the service records and so on.

Be sincere in any apology: As discussed in the previous chapter, if you make any apologies, ensure they are simply that rather than a cloaked deflection or defence.

Unfortunately apologising can be caught up in ego and self-image – areas you may often wish to protect. However, research has shown that when people were first asked to rank their values and personal qualities and to focus on why that value was so important to them, then to write an apology to someone they had hurt but not apologised to, those who had reflected on their values made more sincere, less defensive apologies (Schumann, 2014).

In case you need a quick checklist, Schumann advises that a bad apology:

- Tries to justify your actions
- Blames the recipient
- Makes excuses for the behaviour
- Minimises the consequences.

However, a good apology:

- Acknowledges that you made a mistake/take responsibility for your actions
- Describes what happened and outlines how you will fix the situation
- Pledges to be better next time
- Shows awareness of how you hurt or inconvenienced the recipient

. . . and to make a good apology – should you ever need to – it helps to remind yourself of, and constantly live your organisational values!

Flexibility (the ability to change direction)

Business history is full of examples of companies who came back from the brink to far greater success than prior to their time of crisis, and there are many ways in which you can make such radical changes:

- **Be aware of your customers/clients:** In 2008 Starbucks turned around their fortunes after struggling following rapid growth. The CEO Howard Schultz invited customers to email suggestions for improvement to him and, while he had to close some underperforming stores, they certainly emerged stronger financially. When Old Spice wanted to attract younger purchasers, they brought in NFL player Isaiah Mustafa to promote the campaign during the 2010 Super Bowl. Conversely, both Converse and Doc Martens recognised the power in nostalgia and 'vintage' in turning their sales around.

- **Don't be afraid of a change of management:** Perhaps you need to step down, perhaps someone else, or even a whole team, does. IBM's CEO Lou Gerstner fired nearly 100,000 people in order to change the fortunes of a company losing around $5 billion, to making $81 billion over the course of a 15-year period.

- **Sometimes you need to diversify:** Marvel and Lego are good examples of how entering the world of film helped rejuvenate interest in the comics and toys respectively. Delta managed their financial crisis by making better negotiations with their unions and making internal reforms rather than trying to compete directly with newer airlines.

Unpredictable factors such as inclement weather, or a global pandemic may affect business, but so can competition from the 'faster fish' in your pond.

Try this

▌ Set your senior teams 'thought experiments', e.g. Is our company equipped to cope if a virus such as COVID-19 affected us or our supply chain? Or, how might a tropical sandstorm or adverse weather affect production?

▌ Brainstorm ways in which you could diversify your portfolio – you do not need to follow through, but being aware of your options can be confidence building.

▌ Take regular opportunities to get a sense check of what your customers or clients want – either by asking them for feedback at regular intervals, or through reviewing what you have received from them (ideally both). Even screen your company on social media and see what 'hashtags' are regularly being used alongside your name; and keep abreast of consumer trends within your field.

▌ Always be aware of your finances in case you need to make any unexpected pay-outs.

Engaging with EWoM

Word of mouth has long been a powerful tool to promote trust and loyalty and, because of its reach EWoM has even greater strength (Ismagilova, 2020). Not only do organisations all need an online presence, but also that in itself enables people to reach them and express their views – positive or otherwise.

Ismagilova (2020) has three tips for effective engagement with EWoM.

1. Always respond to customer or client emails. If you do not, it is most likely that the next place they will contact you is the online forum and they may also express their upset with any perceived lack of response. If a client or

customer has gone to a public forum first, invite them to make contact with your organisation directly instead – with people who are able to deal as effectively as possible with their situation.

2. Invite and respond to reviews. Thank the writer for the positive reviews and address any negative ones clearly and concisely. People don't often take the time to say something positive, so by acknowledging them and expressing gratitude you are building relationships. With regards to negative comments, as you will thus be perceived as a responsive organisation, you are most likely to build trust with those who had something nice to say, as well as in comparison with non-responsive businesses. Tucker (2006) defines the concept of 'Transferred trust', which is a client- or customer-generated trust, where organisations may benefit from the lack of trust in competitors, thus looking more trustworthy by comparison.

3. To support receiving more reliable reviews, add a means of rating the review as 'helpful'. This method was employed by Amazon, leading to a jump in profits.

Digital marketing company smallbusinessfuel.com (2020), a group which helps businesses build their understanding and optimisation of their electronic presence, adds:

1. Do your research: Pretend you are your own customer and write down what you might look for in your business. Then make sure your online presence includes those keywords.

2. Be natural and interesting in your 'hashtags': Your clients are human beings and, while hashtags are useful, make sure that your description is still understandable.

3. Post content regularly: Doing this communicates that your website is current and active.

4. Utilise links effectively: Linking with other pages (and benefitting from them linking to you in return) helps improve your ranking in online searches. Guest blogs or collaborative articles can be of use here.

5. Use 'analytics' to find out where your site was accessed from, for how long people viewed and the topics they were interested in.

Also be mindful that while words can be forgotten, your online footprint is hard to erase. While it is possible to pay to have reviews removed, the most effective – albeit time-consuming – method to deal with bad online press is to bump up new, positive, links within search engines (Ronson, 2015). Therefore, make sure you have someone actively engaged with EWoM because your customers, clients, and team will be themselves! . . . and of course, live your positive values daily.

Most of all, remember that 'thinking' is no substitute for action

Even though careful consideration and critical analysis underpin wise actions, actions must still be made. Resilience is about knowing that while you haven't 'rushed in', you can still weather an unexpected outcome, and that taking action potentially also puts you ahead of the curve. Remember that it is often the faster fish that can steal your success, not necessarily the bigger one (Tang, 2016). In the same way as the best actors know their role but always keep half a mind in the present so they can respond to anything unexpected within a live theatre environment, you too must keep an ear to the ground in times of calm, prepare your troops and be ready to seize opportunities when they are presented. The best laid plans must still be executed if they are to work.

END-OF-CHAPTER TOOLKIT

ADOPT Resilience now

Act

Make failure acceptable – as long as you have learned from it.

> *This week:* Encourage your teams to discuss what went
> wrong in previous projects or situations and what they
> have learned or changed. Make it a natural response to
> find out 'What changes will you make next time?' rather
> than turn an admittance of failure into something to
> be reprimanded or ridiculed. (Note that of course this
> depends on the extent of the failure and its consequences,
> but a culture of humiliation if a mistake is made is not
> conducive to building organisational trust.)

Deal

Clear your own 'skeletons' through reflection and reframing.

> *This week:* Are there experiences within your organisational
> or professional history that you are embarrassed over?
> If possible reflect on them and reframe the experience
> into a development one. Take ownership of your role in
> what happened and identify the ways in which you would
> respond differently now.

Optimise

Even if change is not necessary, be aware of the ways in
which you wish to grow.

> *This week:* Start the groundwork of research, networking and
> future planning for the direction you are keen to progress
> in. And be mindful of your planning for potential future
> risk. Do you have procedures in place for emergencies, e.g.
> Flood? Fire? Outbreak? Optimise the work done – see if one
> procedure which is already written could be flexible enough
> to adapt to cover other possible risks.

Prepare

Ensure all your interactions with clients and customers are professionally handled and up to date – try to engage with positive as well as negative feedback.

> *This week:* Very often the tendency is to respond to feedback only to offer explanation when things go wrong. Thanking people for compliments not only encourages their positivity and possibly their loyalty, but it gives the impression that you are a business that engages with others rather than only speaking up to defend yourself.

Thrive

Identify the narratives of resilience within your teams and see if, as an organisation, they can influence your values.

> *This week:* Try this 3-minute activity.
>
> In pairs, ask your teams to spend a minute talking about a time when they have recognised their strength. Ask them to explain what happened and how they got through. Ask the listener to write down words or phrases that seem to be of special significance to the speaker, i.e. words on which they may place extra emphasis while speaking, for example, 'kept going', 'thought about the goal' 'didn't want to let x down'. Then swap. Reflect on what those words or phrases mean, and how you would live them if they became company (or team) values.

Notes

What I did	Date

Reflection (at a later date)

How have my thoughts changed now?

References

Arkes, H. R. and Blumer, C. (1985) The psychology of sunk cost. *Organizational Behavior and Human Decision Processes,* Vol. 35, No. 1, 124–140.

Beaton, C. (2016) This is what happens to your brain when you fail (and how you can fix it), *Forbes* https://www.forbes.com/sites/carolinebeaton/2016/04/07/this-is-what-happens-to-your-brain-when-you-fail-and-how-to-fix-it/#3e215ec31b81 (accessed May 2020).

BSI Group (2017) *Organizational Resilience Index* https://www.bsigroup.com/LocalFiles/zh-tw/organizational-resilience/Index-report-for-web.pdf (accessed May 2020).

Edelstein, J. H. (2019) Good for you, Monica Lewinsky, for finally taking control of your story, *The Guardian* https://www.theguardian.com/commentisfree/2019/aug/08/monica-lewisnky-affair-bill-clinton-tv-series (accessed May 2020).

Ismagilova, E. (2020) *Electronic Word of Mouth.* Conference Presentation, Dubai 2020.

Lewinsky, M. (2015) *The Price of Shame,* TED Talk https://www.ted.com/talks/monica_lewinsky_the_price_of_shame (accessed May 2020).

Ozbay, F., Johnson, D. C., Dimoulas, E., Morgan, C. A., Charney, D. and Southwick, S. (2007) Social support and resilience to stress: From neurobiology to clinical practice. *Psychiatry (Edgmont),* Vol. 4, No. 5, 35–40.

Ronson, J. (2015) *So You've Been Publicly Shamed.* Picador.

Schumann, K. (2014) An affirmed self and a better apology: The effect of self-affirmation on transgressors' responses to victims. *Journal of Experimental Social Psychology,* Vol. 54, 89–96.

Serrat, O. (2009) The Five Whys Technique, *Asian Development Bank* https://www.adb.org/sites/default/files/publication/27641/five-whys-technique.pdf (accessed September 2019).

smallbusinessfuel.com (2020) Top tips when starting a business. *Test the Trend on The Chrissy B Show, Sky 191* https://www.youtube.com/watch?v=nliXlfYQOX8&list=PLHIH0Su1vyzprBHVLkCzOkgvvtk_32tXk&index=2&t=0s (accessed May 2020).

Spear, S. J. (2009) *The High-Velocity Edge*. McGraw Hill.

Suttie, J. (2017) Four ways social support makes you more resilient. *Greater Good Magazine* https://greatergood.berkeley.edu/article/item/four_ways_social_support_makes_you_more_resilient (accessed May 2020).

Tang, A. (2016) *Be A Great Manager Now!* Pearson.

Thalidomide UK (2005) Diageo historical agreement https://www.thalidomideuk.com/diageo-covenant (accessed September 2020).

Tucker, A. (2006) cited in *Guidelines for Measuring Trust in Organizations,* Institute for PR (2016) https://instituteforpr.org/guidelines-for-measuring-trust-in-organizations-2/ (accessed May 2020).

10
Develop a confidence mindset to survive, rebuild and grow

'Unprecedented' was the word of the global pandemic of 2019/2020. A novel coronavirus (COVID-19) rampaged its way across the globe grounding flights, closing businesses and leaving a high human cost in life. Governments scrambled to contain it and protect their nations; businesses had change forced upon them as many were forced to shut their doors or switch to remote working; families were thrown together for school and work as 'social distancing' and quarantine measures were enforced. It was certainly unprecedented, but was everyone also unprepared? What can we learn from crises such as COVID-19 to better strengthen resources and reserves in the case of volatile financial markets, global uncertainty and complex ambiguity?

Complacency can lead to negligence

Reflecting on the initial steps certainly in managing the COVID-19 pandemic, it is arguable that many governments took delayed action. It will not be until much later that we learn the full reasons why. For some it might be a lack of investment in testing kits meant only certain cases were sent to labs; for others, perhaps, there was simply no medical capacity to cope. However, it may also have been a failure to grasp the seriousness of what was going on.

'Hindsight is 2020' as the common saying goes, but those who take time to reflect after being caught short and choose to learn from their mistakes will often put new measures into place to avoid a similar occurrence in the future. This is the reason laws may be changed or passed, or business practices altered permanently. However, although a 'new normal' takes time to get used to, after a duration with little incident there is a human tendency to relax, perhaps overlook things and potentially dismiss warnings that (you may later realise) should have been heeded much earlier.

It is almost as if a very basic model of human error in a crisis can be stated as illustrated below:

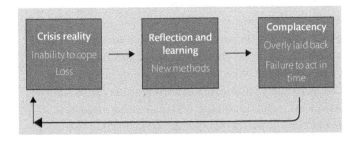

However, it is up to us to be mindful after learning has taken place and **NOT** to fall into the realm of complacency.

Keep a system of regular checks and balances

Ask yourself

▍ Who do you have available to you with whom you know can help you retain a balanced outlook? (This doesn't mean they have to advise you; sometimes simply double checking you have thought things through is enough for the reflective leader.)

▌ How confident are you that your team will challenge your thinking, not to be 'insubordinate', but rather confident in holding an opposing view having thought it through?

▌ How confident are you that you, and your team, think critically and actively when considering information?

▌ How are you continuing to motivate, praise and support your team's growth?

Inspirational leaders are often blessed with eager followers, but without retaining critical thought, it is possible to get swept into complacency with enthusiasm. Psychologist Christopher Bollas said, 'When you have two fully actualised people, their collaboration has the potential to develop a third, newer, bigger approach.' In other words – it is always helpful to have a team that brings their individual insights to the table, *as well as* supporting the vision of the organisation as a whole (Bollas, 1987).

Develop a 'confidence' mindset within your teams

Ask yourself

▌ Do you know the areas in which individuals in your team wish to develop?

▌ Are you aware of the varying skills and abilities your teams have (what are they)?

▌ Does the training that you offer help individuals stretch their skills – and develop new ones?

A host of reasons may prevent teams from asserting their thoughts – culture (organisational and upbringing), previous experience, and simply not knowing that they can. This can result in leaders thinking everyone is 'on the same page', whereas in reality some people are looking for a new job.

Try this

Ask your teams the following, whether in their appraisal time, formally or informally:

▌ What skills would you like to develop to help your own future growth?

▌ What inspires you (and how can we include more of that in our workplace)?

▌ Are there areas of work that you would like to try or learn, even if they are not directly related to what you are doing right now?

. . . and always praise them for what they are doing right now. Building a positive rapport goes a long way to teams feeling confident they can speak up.

A confident mind needs to be nurtured

Providing opportunities for teams to be mentored or supported as they learn new skills can take the fear out of trying something new. Some people choose not to venture outside their comfort zone because of a fear of failure (see Chapter 3). By providing appropriate support – or 'Scaffolding' (Vygotsky, 1978) – in the form of a skilled tutor or mentor, not only will the process of learning become more enjoyable (and more likely to be repeated), but confidence grows as skill does (McCracken, 2017).

The following exercises may also help build confidence from within.

1. Prompt development

Be aware of your team's strengths, and prompt them to keep developing. Keep a matrix which may cover the following key skills of the job, as well as skills (which do not need to be work-related, although they can be) in areas that the team member would like to develop (ideally at least one of those listed must be chosen by the team member themselves):

Name	Key Work Skill 1	KWS 2	KWS 3	KWS 4	Area of Desired Development 1	ADD 2	ADD 3

2. Challenge insecurity

Many people suffer from 'Imposter Syndrome' – the belief that they do not deserve to be there and will 'get found out'. This can sometimes be challenged by encouraging teams to look at (a) what they believe they are inferior to, (b) what they are good at and (c) speaking the truth.

Stamp out inferiority

▌ Try to identify what it is you see in others you deem 'more successful' than you – write it down.

▌ Comparing to a list of your own 'on paper' achievements ask yourself if they are actually better skilled, or if it is their means of expressing their abilities that makes you feel less accomplished. If the latter, consider if you would like to learn that approach; if the former, approach them and ask them their advice on improving skills in that area.

▌ See if you can collaborate with them rather than see yourself in competition. You will either be able to achieve more than you would individually, or you may realise that, in reality, they are not as 'amazing' as you might have believed.

It is often the narrative that you have fashioned that can distort your perceptions, and reframing it can rebuild your self-confidence. Further, acknowledging feelings of envy can help you take control of them – speaking to the person and asking for tips to work towards what they have achieved is more energising than resentment.

Celebrate your own accomplishments and those of others

▌ Young children may be encouraged to write their accomplishments on star-shaped paper and decorate their rooms. There is no reason why adults cannot do the same on Post-its around their desk.

▌ An alternative, if you have a team that knows each other well, is to:

– give each a blank piece of paper and ask them to write their name at the top;

– tell them to pass the paper round and, starting from the bottom, each team member has to write something positive they recognise about the person whose name is at the top of the sheet.

▌ Identify your differences, but also your similarities! A simple Venn diagram may show areas of overlap between your team members or even within departments.

Encourage teams to live (and speak) authentically

Remind teams that it is through speaking their mind (albeit respectfully), that everyone can learn. There is nothing wrong with holding separate points of view, and sometimes much can be learned through hearing another perspective.

3. Work on personal growth and encourage your team to do the same

Find a quiet moment to reflect on your thoughts, opinions and approach to the following self-coaching statements:

- **I try to avoid seeing a challenge to your perception as a threat,** and view it instead as a chance to learn about another point of view.

- **I am the person who seeks to learn constantly,** to try new things, to 'give it a go'. (If you are not – ask yourself why.)

- **I find ways – for example, meditation – to calm and clear my mind.** When your mind is less emotional – or even less rational – we begin to see reality better. Emotion clouds judgement, but so does rigidity to rules or habitual behaviours . . . there may be another solution. Opening the mind to the possibility, by taking a moment (or a day) before we respond, can help . . . 'sleeping on it' can sometimes make a lot of sense if an immediate answer is not needed. This particular tip is key in the very fast-paced world in which we live. We don't have to 'just swipe right' if we don't want to . . . sometimes it's more effective to think on it.

- **I use positive language.** Do you say something is 'good' or 'bad'? If you do, you've weighted it and almost compartmentalised it. Yet that very thing, which was 'bad' (or ineffective) in one context, in a different context may be extremely 'good' (or effective). Embracing the complex fluidity of life, opinion and change through the language we use, while difficult, can help.

- **I always VALIDATE the other person's point of view** before I put my own point across. The purpose of discussion is not necessarily to change someone's mind, but to create potential for both of you to grow. Accepting someone else thinks differently is part of that process.

Model of resilience: Survive–Rebuild–Thrive

In a crisis, 'Survival' can be the hardest part

The model of resilience being used within this book is one of navigating three dips: crisis, exhaustion and competition.

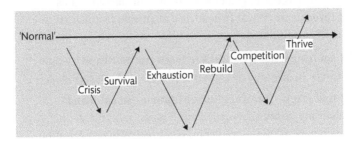

However, when crisis hits, 'survival' brings out the best and the worst in people. When a crisis is unpredictable and not under your own control or containment (such as global disasters), the fight for survival goes beyond your own organisation. You could be fighting for your industry as much as your workplace.

Ask yourself (or reflect)

In a crisis, how will you protect your organisation?

Common survival strategies include the following:

- cost cutting (including redundancies and reducing overheads, downsizing, streamlining business offerings);
- raising or slashing prices of output;
- aggressive marketing techniques.

They are all successful to some degree, but so are what I would call positive or collaborative approaches:

- strengthening relationships with current clients – such as reaching out to ask them specifically how you can better meet their needs;

▌ training (or re-training) can also give your teams a sense of security or at least the confidence that they will be ok should they need to leave at a later point;

▌ focusing on retaining loyal customers – in a situation where everyone is affected, it can be helpful to offer flexibility and understanding to clients who may be struggling.

Reaching out may not always work, but in addition to focusing inwards as the first three strategies suggest, you have given yourself more options for survival – and potential growth through collaboration when things return to a more even keel.

Be mindful of your own behaviours in 'survival' mode

Difficult times are stressful and trying. It is tough to remain positive and often fear and uncertainty can lead to anger, misery and negativity. Be aware that your actions may well be noted by those around you.

Keep a check on yourself that you are:

▌ Role modelling positive behaviour

▌ Not sparking hatred or mistrust

▌ Expressing yourself in ways that are constructive and helpful rather than causing unnecessary unpleasantness

---

Collaboration will often result in faster rebuilding

The strengthening of relationships when times are tough may lead to greater loyalty when they return to normal, and further, a lack of support in hard times will long be remembered. Of course there is always risk to be considered – what if clients are loyal but insolvent, or what if they are forced to change their practice in order to ensure their own survival. It is therefore wise to be aware of your clients and possible partners, and think on their commitment and possible future growth. Recognise also, that the savvy client or partner will be evaluating your potential in the same way.

Your business does not function in a vacuum, and those who will best rebuild are often the ones who made the wisest investments, demonstrated the least offensive behaviour and took the most effective actions during the survival period.

Ask yourself

▌ Of my clients and partners, which of those are most likely to grow with my organisation into the future? (Why and How?)

Note that it may also be worth reflecting on why you think others would not grow with you – you may spot unnoticed potential.

Related to collaboration is the ability to:

▌ Address the realities that your teams are facing – has the crisis caused them financial hardship which affects their quality of life? It would be inappropriate and ineffective to push them to meet targets if they are struggling to repay their mortgage.

▌ Work out ways in which new systems can be of global benefit. If you struggled with communication or supply chains during a crisis, what measures can be implemented globally to ease this in future? If during the crisis you changed your way of working, for example, working from home, would retaining those systems help regrowth, e.g. through reducing overheads or making space for developments which cannot be implemented remotely such as the creation of large work-related facilities or hubs?

▌ Be aware of your ethical practices. Do any of your systems that need an overhaul afford the opportunity to move to a healthier means of achieving aims?

Thriving after crisis

As you begin to grow again, learn from what went before. If you are pursuing new directions and are stopping certain offerings, make sure that you are not trimming off too much.

1. Don't trim too much

Ask yourself

▌ How 'LEAN' should lean be?

A reasonable reason for cuts is to avoid wastage. If something is recognised as non-cost-effective, it is soon phased out. Unfortunately on the occasion that the unexpected does occur, this can leave you wanting.

While it is not always necessary to retain something that no longer has constant use, it is wise to consider the following:

Mini 'risk assessment'

▌ How would I access a withdrawn item or service should it be needed?

This may include thinking about relationships you need to build or maintain as well as training that may need to occur.

▌ What mitigating factors are in place to ensure no great loss is suffered if I do not have this withdrawn item or service?

▌ How great is my risk if I do not have this withdrawn item or service should I come to need it?

> Always ensure that the solution remains
> more helpful than the problem was
> troublesome

2. Reconnect and welcome

Reconnect with organisations you may have lost touch with during the time of crisis, being sensitive to where they are in terms of their regrowth.

Also, nurture the new partnerships that formed, especially if they look mutually beneficial.

3. Be aware of the 'pulse' of your clients, customers and teams

When a crisis has lifted, many people will have been affected and many may have gone through their own process of change. For some they will welcome the chance to 'return to normal', others may have taken a new path that they find suits them and others may have been very overwhelmed and are simply struggling to stand again. Be sensitive to the changing needs – even if you are not able to meet them all.

4. Keep the 'coping strategies' that proved to be more effective than previous practice

COVID-19 saw pollution reduce in many countries as aeroplanes were grounded, and fewer vehicles were on the road. Remote working became normalised, and hygiene practices took centre stage. Some of these factors resulted in greater productivity as well as employee work–life balance. Remember that I said at the beginning of this book – resilience is not simply about returning, it is about growing.

Working from home became a common occurrence and many businesses remained in contact through online platforms such as Zoom or Microsoft Teams. Even Facebook and WhatsApp got in on the 'private meeting room' act. But after the initial excitement wore off came a sense of exhaustion.

As a consultant who also sees clients from home, these are my tips for avoiding 'online meeting' fatigue:

Do not schedule back-to-back meetings

- I know this is harder when you are co-ordinating different departments and teams, but ask your teams too whether they have a gap between connections. With meetings 'in real life', a natural break, perhaps to drive or walk from one to the other, was built in, and this gave you time to clear your head. Even in my book *The Leader's Guide to Mindfulness*, I suggested that you do a 'mental palate cleanse' (like the water biscuit between wine tastings to clear the mouth) – doing star jumps, running on the spot or splashing a bit of cold water on your face between meetings allows you to enter the next one refreshed and better able to concentrate from the start.

- 'Back-to-back' online meeting is efficient, but when it doesn't allow for a chance to clear one's head, is it really effective?

- As a coach I would never schedule clients directly one after the other – whether online or in my office – because it is extremely exhausting to give your full attention to one person and switch to the next. Someone will lose out, most likely you. The same is true of your teams (and you as both chair and on behalf of your organisation if your team is exhausted). At the very least I put in a 30-minute gap, and that's short considering meetings can over-run. You don't call a meeting just for fun – you owe it to yourself, your team and your business to be fully present when discussing the issues important enough to meet over.

▌ Ask yourself if it needs to be done in an online meeting room

– Will a phone call do? Will a text message be short and sweet enough? Online meetings take energy. I request them if I cannot see clients in person because I need to be able to look at their body language . . . your body language can betray a lot, and through that I am better able to 'probe' certain topics or focus on certain areas. But I think it is only fair that in turn my client sees me. They don't need to read my body language, but it is wholly appropriate that they are reassured they have my full attention.

– That's another problem with online meetings – as with those in the physical boardroom – you *do* have to be present. It is therefore more exhausting. If you can get the information across effectively in a different format, consider it.

– A recorded webinar or class can, as long as you don't need to see your students, mean that they can access it whenever they want – and that enables them to manage their time (and you to manage yours if it's just yourself and a camera).

▌ Mind your manners

– You are working from home – that means, unless you have a completely separate home office (and even then), you are still inviting others into *your house.* This can feel like an intrusion. Also, because you are at home in an environment that is often connected with relaxation, be aware that you are not being too casual, or that if you are rude or critical, how others may feel taking that in their personal space.

– In *Be A Great Manager Now!*, I suggested that when resolving conflict it is best done on neutral territory so that no-one feels threatened. Now, in the context of work not only are you inviting colleagues with whom you wouldn't necessarily have a drink with into your home, but you are also entering theirs. (Dressing for the occasion is therefore recommended.)

▌**Children, pets, post arriving, WIFI connections and other issues are a fact of 'WFH' life**

If you are that worried, apologise from the start, and use it as an opportunity later to speak with your children and talk about your work and what they can do to stay occupied if you are on a call, but be mindful of making them too afraid to interrupt in case there is an emergency.

▌**To record or not to record**

This can supplement minute taking. If you are recording though, let everyone know, and consider giving them permission to record too. However, be very aware of confidentiality and privacy regulations regarding recording, storage and use.

▌**Get some offline time**

– Switch off, go out into the garden, or at least open a window. Get some time away from the glare of the screen (and all the lighting you might be using to work your 'on camera' look).

Take a moment to be informally mindful:

– Listen to the birds

– Feel the warmth of the sun

– Breathe deeply

– Read (a book rather than a download), sing, draw – do something away from a screen

– Enjoy a cup of tea (or your choice of beverage) – really enjoy it

– Use an eye mask to get some rest.

5. Celebrate, praise and thank your team

While it may be a relief to come through a difficult period, make sure you find time to celebrate with your team for doing what they had to do. It is not easy to comply when restrictions or changes are imposed for outcomes which are not immediately visible and the support and trust that will have been placed in you must be recognised. This also includes people such as site managers whose roles may not have previously been seen as so important. If you can, take the time to thank individuals in person, or at the very least 'personally'.

END-OF-CHAPTER TOOLKIT

ADOPT Resilience now

Act

Ensure a learning mindset. Even when things are running effectively and efficiently, continue to broaden your knowledge and keep your mind active. When in a tight spot it is often quick, creative thinking that is the most effective path to success. Bioengineers at Stanford University invented a malaria test made out of a string and two pieces of card. Based on the 'whirly-gig' toy, they had created a centrifuge which would go on to support developing populations (Newby, 2017).

> *This week:* Set mini-challenges to stretch the creative capabilities of your teams. Avoid placing them under extra pressure, but find enjoyable ways to engage – and recognise – their creativity.

Deal

Listen when dissenting voices raise concerns about cuts. It takes courage – and the creation of the receptive environment emphasised at the start of this chapter – to speak up. Applaud their efforts through acknowledging them.

> *This week:* If concerns are raised over an organisational decision – even one that has not been set out for consultation, take a moment if you can, to see for yourself why your team may be concerned.

Optimise

Encourage your teams to voice concerns and speak their mind. Have a number of channels through which they can reach you, and remember that sometimes people need more direct prompting than 'my door is always open'.

This week: Ask your teams any of the reflective development questions at the start of this chapter, or build them into pre-planned appraisal time.

Prepare

While it is not essential to raise alarm, keep yourself aware of the growing global issues. Sex discrimination, sexual harassment and mental health are as much at the forefront of people's concerns as climate change. The next crisis may never arise in your lifetime . . . but what if it does? Remember, resilience is best built *before* the point of crisis.

This week: Read a non-field article on a global issue.

Thrive

Crises always bring a human cost, but they also present the best of human strength. This original poem reminds us that thriving is as much about remembering to live again as much as succeed:

> 'And when this is all over
> We'll knock on our friends' doors
> And go to every party
> And say "I love you" more.
>
> 'And when this is all over
> Through bad we'll see the good

➤

> Because whenever we are together
> We'll appreciate it, as we should.
>
> 'And when this is all over
> And we are no longer in this pain
> We'll know to never take for granted
> Those little things again.'
>
> (published by Jasmine O'Dell, **https://www.jasmineodell.com/**)

Notes

What I did	Date

Reflection (at a later date)

How have my thoughts changed now?

References

Bollas, C. (1987) *The Shadow of the Object: Psychoanalysis of the thought unknown.* Free Association Books.

McCracken, M. (2017) 5 skills to learn if you want to be more confident (yes confidence can be learned), *Inc.* https://www.inc.com/mareo-mccracken/want-to-be-more-confident-5-leadership-habits-to-start-right-now.html (accessed May 2020).

Newby, K. (2017) Inspired by a whirligig toy: Stanford bioengineers develop a 20-cent, hand-powered blood centrifuge, *Stanford News* https://news.stanford.edu/2017/01/10/

whirligig-toy-bioengineers-develop-20-cent-hand-powered-blood-centrifuge/ (accessed May 2020).

O' Dell, J. (2020) *Poetry in Isolation* https://www.jasmineodell.com/ (accessed September 2020).

Vygotsky, L. S. (1978) Interaction between learning and development. In M. Cole, V. John-Steiner, S. Scribner and E. Souberman (Eds.) *Mind and Society: The development of higher psychological processes* (pp. 79–91). Harvard University Press.

Resilient future planning

Question: Would you change anything if you could do it all again?

My answer: No, but I'd probably get myself a bit more mentally fit for it!

(Rodgers and Marshall, 2020)

'You never know how strong you are until you are tested'

This is an oft-spoken sentiment – especially when mental, physical and emotional testing is hitting us without reprieve. Some are strong – still standing, coping, working it out – but were they simply born that way? One thing I have always held constant is that I wouldn't change anything I have been through (even the tough experiences) because it has all made me who I am, *but* I do sometimes wish I'd built up a better emotional fitness base earlier.

Three components of resilience

As you will have seen throughout this book, resilience is about first of all surviving the crisis, then rebuilding after it and finally thriving. This requires three key components:

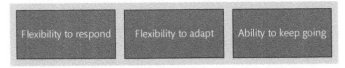

| Flexibility to respond | Flexibility to adapt | Ability to keep going |

Ask yourself

Now, in your current mindset, having reached the final chapter:

- How easy is it for you to adapt? (We may think we are flexible, but what if someone requires you to do something you're really not keen on. Will you do it if you have to? But, more importantly, will you do it WELL?)

- How quickly do you learn (I don't mean 'pick up new skills', I mean change habits that have grown over the years)? And do you stick at it when it's tricky?

- How likely is it that you can keep going – even if you have to adapt again and then learn even more in the process?

You have the tools, you have the learning, but you need to be able to persevere when times are challenging, and that is the true test of resilience. Remember that motivation depends largely on two things:

1. Your personal preference within the options available.
2. The expectation you can do it, and that it will bring about results.

By continually broadening your thinking you will often discover or create more options, and the more you practise, the more likely that you will be able to do it and that it will work. But you need to trust yourself to do it. The role of a coach, trainer – and of course leader – is not to give teams a 'quick fix', but to instill within them the knowledge that they can create or execute their own 'fix' whenever they need it, whatever life throws at them. Therefore, as this book begins its conclusion, I would like you to think about your strengths and support outside these pages.

Ask yourself

'Who and/or what strengthens your trust in you? Who and what helps you keep on keeping on?'

▮ These are the people who share your values and energise you when you meet.

▮ They are the mentors and teachers, with whom you don't mind showing the vulnerability of 'being bad at it' – and listening to them to improve.

▮ These are the 'little things' in life that keep you going – noticing the pleasantness of a taste, a sound, smell, touch.

▮ They may be mental exercises you do – much like physical ones – that keep your brain flexible.

This may be the most important element of all in resilience, and it may also be the only one which you struggle with if you believe you must 'go it alone'.

The problem with taking any action is – you don't always get a response.

Somebody to lean on

I have a soft spot for 'inspirational films' – the ones where people grow from seemingly impossible situations. Of course I understand that 'dramatic license' is taken, but there are some things which seem true in all stories of rising through the ashes:

▮ Ability to learn (albeit after a few false starts!)

▌ Ability to adapt

▌ *Support from someone or something.*

What I find is often underplayed in such films, is the protagonist's trust in themselves above all that. Somehow, they know they will cope – and the support they get from the other – the mentor, the friend, the trainer – is something that helps them stay strong in that trust.

'Knowing you will cope' is essential, because life is not rewarded in the same way as school may have been. The 'rules' are unclear, you won't always get a 'gold star' – and sometimes you have no idea if what you are doing is making any difference at all; unless you look out for it yourself, and then you may not get any form of praise or acknowledgement for it.

Therefore, the ability to keep going is often based on trust.

And the trust that you will carry on is often best strengthened by *support from someone or something.*

A point of warning, however – you cannot transfer all your trust into an external source. *The external source (friend, teacher, mentor, religion) is there to keep you keep going.* You need to be in the driving seat, but it's difficult to continue when you're feeling lost. Hence, the external source helps restore your verve – it does not become it. And certainly, if you are lucky enough to have faith through someone's belief in you – remember to thank them. They didn't need to give you their time (and even if you were paying them (e.g. a coach or consultant), the most inspirational will have had traits that go beyond the 'going rate' for their hard skills . . . such as encouragement, praise, recognition that you were worthy). While life is indeed 'what *you* make of it' – these are the very people who will have helped make you – *you.*

'The traitor appears not a traitor' – Rebuilding is sometimes harder than survival

> *'An enemy at the gates is less formidable, for he is*
> *known and carries his banner openly. But the traitor*
> *moves amongst those within the gate freely, his sly*
> *whispers rustling through all the alleys, heard in the*
> *very halls of government itself. For the traitor appears*
> *not a traitor'*

> (Taylor Caldwell)

Be aware that 'survival mode' is engaged at the time when energy reserves are the highest. Further, with adrenaline often at an all-time high during this period, and the single-minded focus to 'get through', without being struck down directly by the crisis itself, it is often possible to drag yourself out the other side as difficult as it is. As the case with global pandemics, climate change or financial bubbles bursting, the enemy, as Taylor Caldwell describes '. . . is known and carries his banner openly'. It is the aftermath that follows the relief of survival, which in some cases may lead to 'survivor guilt', in others 'post-traumatic stress'. In many it will be debt along with an entire disruption of what was happening pre-crisis, as well as the almost desperate desire to 'get back to where you were', that can be the biggest cause of depression. Financial depressions are common after a crisis – physical, emotional and mental exhaustion is not far behind – after all, you have worked to survive. Now you get no rest and you must rebuild.

Worse still you must do so at a time when everyone is struggling to get back on their feet. There is greater competition and often less patience for sharing or helping as there was during the crisis. Measures that might have helped you during survival mode now need to be repaid at a time where there is still a shortage of opportunity – but an even greater shortage of charity.

Resilience must not only prepare you for survival, but for the aftermath and the two dips that follow – rebuilding through exhaustion and then thriving past competition. Your mental and emotional fitness must be at a peak, and this is why you are regularly reading (and hopefully utilising the techniques within) this book.

Ask yourself

Before or during the survival period

▌ What or who keeps you going when you are exhausted?

▌ How can you take or find respite while in a period of crisis?

▌ What is the minimum you need during the crisis stage in order to survive? (Thus leaving less to repay, restore or rebuild.)

During the rebuild period

▌ Who or what of your new collaborations can assist with your restoration?

▌ What renewed, revisited or transferrable skills can now be utilised?

And do a regular 'sense check' on the consumer and client climate, exploring new areas or opportunities where possible.

When able to thrive

▌ Have all the exposed weaknesses been addressed satisfactorily?

▌ What lessons were learned and how can they inform your current decisions?

▌ Have you shown appreciation to all those who came together to pull through to this point, and do you continue to do so?

There is little time to stop. Life is simply a journey where the vehicle may accelerate, brake, take a wrong turn or even have an accident – but it doesn't cease.

You need to have the fitness to carry on.

Resilience is largely preparation – *before* you need to be tested

It's filling up the tank and checking the oil at the start of your journey, only you're often doing it on the move, and you don't know when you'll need it the most. Resilience is about being ready to go faster, to swerve corners, to brake but not crash. You have to be revved up but know how to drive regardless of terrain. Therefore, it is about *building and constantly topping up* emotional and mental *fitness and* not necessarily about 'perfect health'.

Resilience is the knowledge that you *can and will cope* BEFORE the act of proving it, and the best time to work on it is when things are calm. When they are not, you need all that emotional and mental energy you *have* built up to survive and rebuild! As I said in Chapter 9, it is the knowledge that you *will be ok*, that you can and will cope in all three stages of resilience rather than the act of proving it. You will also find that if you have built up your strength, not only is survival and rebuilding easier, but you are already better placed to find ways to thrive following the unexpected.

It is never too early nor too late to build resilience

Try these

The ABC building blocks

These three tips come from Dialectical Behaviour Therapy, used very effectively to help people manage and work with their emotions. As with any form of building resilience they are most effective when done before a crisis, as they are much harder to find time to do when in 'survival mode'. It's hard work, but think of emotional fitness like physical fitness – the more you practise, the better you get!

➤

A = Accumulate positive experiences

Professional

▌ **Hold team days, socials or activities** that allow people to interact on a casual basis.

Personal

▌ **Spend more time with people who make you feel positive** and less with those who bring you down (this may mean muting, blocking or unfollowing some accounts on social media – even if it's temporarily).

General

▌ **When you are doing something you enjoy, focus on it consciously.** Last Christmas I set a 'Conscious Christmas Challenge' giving people £5 to spend consciously rather than habitually handing over a card and forgetting what they bought. One person bought 'The best £5 beer ever!'. I think it was a large and overpriced 'artisan' beer at a known tourist spot, but he really enjoyed it – and that's exactly what it was about!

▌ **Actively seek to do things you like.** This may mean revisiting once-loved hobbies or skills that daily life has shelved.

▌ **Recognise the value in the little things you already have** – a beautiful day (even out of the window), a pet curled up on your lap (happening as I type), tastes, smells, sounds and textures which you might otherwise take for granted. This goes for the people you value in your life too – tell them, often.

B = Build mastery

Professional

▌ **Learn to stretch your comfort zones every day.** This doesn't mean making huge leaps forward, but just focus on being a little bit better today than you were yesterday! Enter teams in competitions, or set team challenges that are fun but also stretching their talents.

Personal

▌ **Remind yourself of what makes you proud of you.** I tell my younger 'clients' to write down all the things that make them special in pretty shapes and look at it often – you might want to do that on a few Post-its!

General

▌ **Do something that makes you feel accomplished.** I'm all for encouraging you outside your comfort zones, but sometimes, when you're in a tricky patch and you have to find the strength to pick up and start again, doing something you're already good at can remind you that you *can* do it. **It's not the actual skill that counts, but the reminder that you know in yourself that you can learn, you do work hard and you will get there.**

C = Cope ahead

Professional

▌ While you cannot plan for every eventuality, how prepared are you for the situations that are foreseeable? If there is something that has caught you out in the past, learn from it and **have an action plan**. You may never need to use it, so it doesn't always need to be much more than awareness of how you might respond, but that very act of priming your mind means it is more likely to swing into action should the need arise.

Personal

▌ **Have a list of 'useful numbers'** ready and be aware of who can help you should you need it. In doing so, perhaps spend a moment strengthening those relationships positively. Collaboration is key to survival, regrowth and thriving beyond. Who is in your network, and can you rely on them? Then ask – how can you help each other?

General

▌ **Make regular 'sense checks'** – be aware not just of your immediate environment, but of the wider one. In a business this means not just your field, but how the global zeitgeist is moving and begin future-proofing. What training might you need? What adaptations could you start to consider now?

Remember, crisis doesn't always cause issues – but it will reveal cracks

The stress and strain of a crisis doesn't automatically mean that everything you have worked for is doomed to fail, but the weak links will be exposed.

The best time to look at these – many practical ways of doing so are included throughout this book – is before the crisis hits. Unfortunately this is the very time that the mindset of 'it's not broke, don't fix it' or 'we can relax now' can be the root of the eventual problem.

One of the dangers of resting too long on laurels, especially following a period of tumultuous or difficult change, is that there is a fine line between coping *to* confidence *to* complacency.

When you have come through as a survivor, it is common for confidence to build – the mindset of 'Thank goodness' can soon turn to 'That wasn't so bad', and unless you remain mindful of your actions, this can result in making choices based on a situation that no longer exists. For example, some crises lead to the act of 'panic buying'. Many researchers would discuss the psychology of the 'panic' or 'hoarding' mindset, but few looked at the perspective of the retailer. As the pace of society has quickened, consumer behaviour has changed with it, and one such change saw fewer people buying a 'monthly shop' in favour of 'popping round the corner to pick up . . .'. Retailers responded to that demand – they became more efficient, but 'Highly efficient systems have no slack, no redundancy and therefore no resilience and no spare capacity. That's a problem because perfect conditions rarely exist for long in the real world, and "rare" events happen more often than you would think.'(Lewis, 2020). As I said in the last chapter – be mindful how 'lean is lean'. Remain responsive, and remain alert, whatever your pathway forward.

> You may be hit unexpectedly, but you don't need to put the 'jerk' into knee jerk

Conduct an organisational 'fitness check' at regular intervals

Use downtime (time outside crisis) to keep an ear to the ground and an eye on how your organisation is growing.

Try this

Note that while this is most likely to happen after a crisis, this is best repeated regularly.

Audit your areas of weakness

1. **Reflect on and correct areas of weakness in your initial response stages.** While the same occurrence may not happen again in your lifetime, you may have identified certain areas in which your response was sluggish or affected company morale and trust. Be aware of what happened, through asking the **'5 whys'** (asking 'why' five times to get to the root cause of the problem – see Chapter 9).

2. **Know that intellectual awareness is NOT the same as practical preparation.** It's all very well knowing the 'theory' of what you might do, but it is action that is essential. In life coaching terms, I tell over-thinking clients 'don't be the most enlightened person that never lived'. You need to be able to put those ideas into practice, and if you cannot, then work to adapt them so you can.

3. **Are there wider opportunities or networks with whom you can grow collaboratively?** Use this time to network or reach out to explore opportunities especially since you have been afforded time to think, as well as holding the awareness that people's habits and behaviours may change after a crisis. Consider also previous areas of expertise which may even be 'Now defunct' – would their revival

➤

serve you well? Skills are never wasted, they are simply like an itinerary – you are using what works best for you at the time; but it doesn't mean they've disappeared, even if they now require a little brushing up.

4. **Be aware of changing consumer/client behaviours.** Following a crisis or changed situation, the lifestyle we had been used to may change and so our consumer behaviour may follow. Organisations need to keep abreast of and consider the possible mindset of their clients and customers.

5. **Use the time to reflect on your own responsiveness and growth potential.** Here are some questions to ask yourself if you have been gifted some quiet time:

- If you knew a disruption or crisis would last longer than the proposed 12 weeks, how might you respond?

- If you knew 6 months ago this would happen how would you prepare?

- What long-term strategic projects may have to change or could be started as a result?

- With whom can you collaborate to help you with any changes of direction, or to help each other rebuild after financial loss or other negative effects?

6. **Be mindful of your 'fear responses'?.** Crisis brings fear, and fear can result in knee-jerk reactions. Be aware of what yours are so that you do not fall back into old habits. You would not drink poison if you were thirsty, why would you engage in toxic practices just because you are afraid?

Finally start getting your mental and emotional wellbeing into shape by trying these simple things – right now:

Choose one of the following to focus on each week and rotate them until you are doing all three comfortably:

1. **Learn widely** – this may be focused on your industry, your personal development, your family, your interests – it is not specifically goal oriented. The idea is, you become used to considering many ideas and viewpoints.

2. **Be aware you are making active choices** - behaviour does not have to be habitual. If you find something is, when you get a moment ask yourself why and what alternatives you may have available. This keeps your mindset flexible.

3. **Try it - whatever 'it' is.** You don't always need to be asked (in fact, if you are an 'instigator' that's quite a skill because many often prefer to follow). You also don't need to try it with anyone else - if you want to do it, do it, why wait for someone to hold your hand? This builds your confidence that you can do it, if you must, on your own.

Resilience – or at least building mental and emotional fitness *prior to being* tested – will always serve you well (even if crisis doesn't come just yet). Your behaviour now may also role model how those who come after you will respond – something which can be the turning point on how your legacy will continue. Resilience is a skill for life as important as physical strength and financial security – and remember, living isn't even like running a 'marathon', it's surviving, building and thriving for a *lifetime!*

Start your engine

Your final toolkit consists of two activities. The first is aimed at boosting your ability to survive and rebuild, reminding you of what you have and where you have come from. The second is to support your growth and vision to thrive.

TEAM CHARTERED TERRITORY – the storyboard roadmap

This activity, adapted from Rodgers and Marshall (2020) can be done as a 'road map' style picture collage with photographs being used to represent the answer.

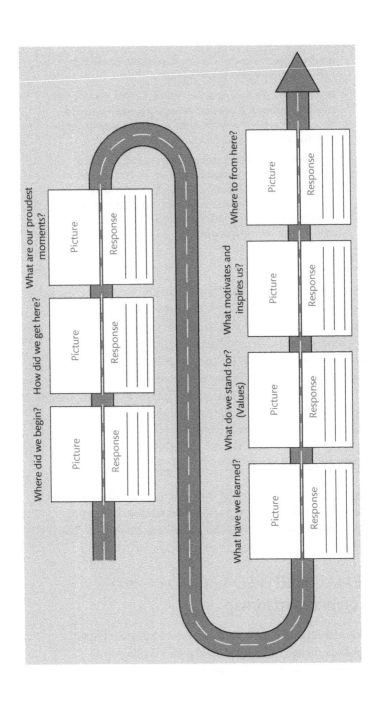

This storyboarded roadmap serves as a reminder to keep a team strong and focused during the period of crisis and the rebuilding aftermath. The focus on values (a current theme throughout this book) is key in continuing to move forward because that, hopefully, speaks to what is deemed purposeful and meaningful and justifies the hard work. This can even be kept as a display or a screensaver and, rather than change it, subsequent ones can be created to continue the journey of growth.

TEAM UNCHARTERED COURSE – the vision board

With your team, identify:

- Your overall goal.
- Three words that capture your everyday values (NOT a mission statement, but what you aim to do every day).
- The ideal clients/customers/contracts you wish to attract.
- The financial bottom line for the year (and what you aspire to).
- The key collective team behaviours.
- With whom you would like to work/build/maintain relationships – and why.
- The key skills you wish to acquire (whether through outsourcing or upskilling).
- Your ideals/motivational quotes.

You may set this out as a wall collage with images, and change it as priorities change, but it will give you a collective goal to focus on as you continue to grow.

Final thoughts

Building your resilience, that is your mental and emotional fitness (which in turn reflects in your physical and hard skills performance), is not something you can easily do at the point of crisis, yet this is the most common time to seek out consultants, coaches – or even to buy this book perhaps. Yet, you will benefit far more if you start doing it beforehand, even slowly. In the same way as any fitness trainer will tell you that you cannot maintain an athlete's frame without regular work, you need to build your energy reserves (or 'top up your energy tank') to maintain a healthy outlook in order to keep going when things get tough.

However, it is never too late – nor too early – to start.

Build your resilient future now.

END-OF-CHAPTER TOOLKIT

ADOPT Resilience now

Act

Make whatever you've changed stick but adding more of the good rather than restricting the bad. Remember that it is not just the behaviour that has to change, but the mindset. To 'lose a stone' you can, with discipline restrict your diet and raise your exercise intake, but to maintain it you need to think like someone a stone lighter. Restrictions and discipline work best short term, it is the lifestyle change that counts, but it is much harder. Instead I would recommend, once you are maintaining a weight loss, to add more of the healthy behaviours; for example, a regular exercise plan, drinking a specific amount of water, eating a certain amount of fruit and veg, which may leave less room for the unhealthy ones such as eating junk food.

This week: Seek to *add more* of the positive behaviours you have engaged in while reading this book. Make time for reflection, or gratitude, or training, and there may be less left over for worrying about areas which you have no influence over.

Deal

If you are going to direct your energy somewhere, make it count. Following on from the point above, if you have decided to focus on an area of concern, ensure it is one that you can influence, and then seek to influence it. Sometimes, as a way of making us feel less 'guilty' when things are running smoothly, our minds wander to things we cannot influence so that we still sustain a sense of worry.

This week: Divide your areas of concern into what you can influence and what you cannot, and take action over at least one of the points within your influence.

Optimise

Reflect on the learning in every situation. I was a drama teacher before I returned to academic psychology, and during that time through lessons and productions I know I embedded discipline, teamwork, camaraderie, and many life skills – some students learned that, others simply learned drama.

This week: No matter what you are doing, personal or professional, seek to learn something either about yourself or about behaviour within that situation. Baking with children can teach you about managing for unpredictable outbursts of creativity, learning a skill can teach you about your focus. Everything is an opportunity to grow – seize it.

Prepare

Be realistic in what you have to do. In any goal you decide to undertake, be clear on:

▌ What you need to do

▌ Your current level of skill in that area

▌ Your next steps to improvement.

Whether you do this formally through a coaching wheel where you:

▌ Identify your areas of focus

▌ Indicate on a scale of 1–10 where your skill level rests

▌ Set out an action plan to move that scale at least one notch up in each area.

Or if you simply make a note, know where you are, what you need to do – and do it.

> *This week:* Identify your next goal – and take one small step towards it.

Thrive

Sometimes it can feel like a thankless task – but if you believe in it, keep going. So often you may ask yourself 'Is it worth it?' Perhaps you have been striving for ages for a specific client to notice you or for a promotion or longed for development in your business. You have worked, you have done all your personal development, and you still feel as far away as when you started. Remember that you don't need *everyone* to see you, just *the right one* (and the 'right one' may not be who you had considered at the outset). To stay strong, look instead at the smaller wins. Look at the times your team has said 'thank you'; smile at their achievements under your leadership; bask in the warmth and comfort of the positive environment your actions have created in your life and relationships in your corner of the world. It's worth it.

This week: Just keep going.

Notes

What I did	Date

Reflection (at a later date)

How have my thoughts changed now?

References

Caldwell, T. (1983) *A Pillar of Iron*. Fawcett.

Lewis, H. (2020) How panic buying revealed the problem with the modern world, *The Atlantic* https://amp.theatlantic.com/amp/article/608731/?_gsa=1 (accessed May 2020).

Rodgers, C. and Marshall, N. (2020) Welcome Break International Women's Day Keynote, Newport Pagnell.

Epilogue: Resilient leadership

We will all leave a legacy. What will yours be? How long will it last? And what impact will it have?

That choice is yours.

Resilient practice will enable you to appreciate the world as it is, while recognising that it doesn't always have to remain that way. It will allow you to embrace vulnerability as it gives way to compassion and kindness, while being able to withstand failure or disappointment. Growth through learning and flexibility is always more robust than standing completely rigid, no matter how solid you are – it gives you the strength to succeed *because* of your excellence, and sustain *in spite* of your shortfalls. Perhaps it may even be seen as the 'flip' side of the Buddhist approach to mindfulness – where acceptance of suffering and accumulation of knowledge result in liberation.

Use the techniques you have learned in this book to make lasting changes in the areas that you choose, rather than watching from the side lines, or simply responding. Motivate those whom you support – and value, or seek them out to collaborate with them in engaging with joined growth. Resilience empowers you to think more clearly and choose more wisely, even under pressure and the need for adaptability – because you are confident in yourself. Use what you have learned to start charting your path.

Remember also that resilience sits hand in hand with mindfulness. (My previous book *The Leader's Guide to*

Mindfulness presents you with another series of practical applications. These are rooted in the Buddhist practice now popular in business culture and proven to produce real results in wellbeing personally and professionally.) Mindfulness helps us get off the automated treadmill of life and move from 'human *do*ings' to 'human *be*ings' (Rev. Mandy Marriott, 2020). By *be*ing, we are better able to recognise our values, our needs, our goals. We recognise what around us is important to nurture and what we can simply release so it no longer burdens us – leaving us the space and energy to channel into achieving our true desires. However, coupled with building resilience – the drive to set positive foundations, to grow strength, and to thrive – that enlightenment becomes the starting point to take positive action, but this time in a directed, focused and fundamentally significant manner. Rather than simply doing, mindfulness broadens our minds to be; with resilience as the aim, we can do again – just better.

Indeed, we are always better motivated when we know what we want to do, and how to do it. Lawler (1994) said that our motivation is based on two things: our preference for the choices in front of us; and the expectation that we (a) can do it and (b) we'll get the results. You will notice that all the exercises in this book, while urging you to action, are underpinned by thought.

Building resilience brings greater rewards than saving money on PR, or good marketing, or 'attracting Millennials' – because:

1. It means survival and longevity – even through the tough times. This may be because you have embedded values in your current team, perhaps through them you attract others who can help, and with a flexible mindset perhaps adaptation has been smoother – and even prepared for.

2. It keeps you mentally and emotionally strong enough to rebuild after crisis. Even though your team may be exhausted, even though they may have had to adapt, and even though it may still be some time before you see the fruits of your labour, you trust in your methods and in yourselves to keep going.

3. It enables you to thrive. Because you have been *living* and *taking control* of your course in a pro-active manner, you are ready and may even be prepared to seize opportunities or innovate ideas – maybe even having a range of options to see which blossom. If you are merely responsive, you will always be catching up.

Take effective action

Resilient thinkers are taking action ahead of the curve – or, if they have been 'caught short' – they are swift to make the necessary changes and then improve on their competitor. The growth of both Zoom and Google Meet during the 2020 pandemic is a great example of the latter already having the software in place and learning from the bubble of the former; but the lack of available testing in favour of ventilators is an example of not learning from the countries with lowest cases and fearing competition from those seemingly 'bigger' – research from the United States soon questioned the use of ventilators as related to significantly high death rates, and the Nightingale Hospitals went to standby almost before they got started – remember, don't be the 'jerk' of knee jerk.

Make wise choices

You may find, especially after crisis, that things will have changed. Where you may have had to hurriedly put contingency plans into place, now you can stop and reflect on what will work long term – the new long term.

For example, it is all very well that organisations may eventually turn to a 'work from home' model to reduce overheads, or higher education may move to greater online classes which may in turn provide better knowledge sharing, collaborations and opportunity – but always future plan. Rather than rush into buying technology, consider what the use will be; how it might develop; and how easy it is to integrate into your current systems. Resilience is about addressing all possibilities – and taking a mindful pause in order to do so in the manner that will yield greatest results – or at least allow for flexibility should the unexpected occur again. While you cannot predict everything, you can be prepared to adapt.

Look after your wellbeing

Do not underestimate the importance of 'topping up your energy tank'. Structure in time for you – whether that is to pursue activities that make you feel accomplished; or which relax you; or simply make you feel good. The more energised you are, the better your performance.

And finally, go with good GRACE

I would like to leave you with an exercise from my coaching sessions which will enable you to underpin all your actions with the best parts of mindfulness (the head), resilience (the gut) and compassion (the heart) – our three key drivers:

- **G**ather Attention: Before you make a decision, make an effort to focus on this act. Do not sell yourself short through distraction.

- **R**ecall Intention: Remember your values and ensure they underpin that choice. What is it that you were intending to do – and will this action achieve those ends?

▌ **Attune to what is relevant:** Do a mental 'risk assessment' – attend to the cautions and concerns that are relevant, be aware of the others, but do not let them affect your choices.

▌ **Consider what is best for all concerned:** Always remember those within your teams, communities or wider networks on whom you may wish or need to rely.

▌ **Engage and Enact:** Do it.

(GRACE Model by Halifax; cited in Gilbert and Choden, 2014)

> Resilience means: No matter your past, you can own your present and create your future if you reflect, reframe and rewrite

Resilience is within the core of you and your organisation, rather than something additional. It starts within and extends out through what you do, how you do it and who you do it with. Know your values, address your weaknesses and set your goals, then do the same for those of your organisation, and go out and live them, interconnectedly, successfully and sustainably within the teams, communities and networks around you.

References

Gilbert, P. and Choden (2014) *Mindful Compassion*. New Harbinger Publications.

Lawler, E. E. (1994) *Motivation in Work Organizations*. Wadsworth Publishing Co Inc.

Marriott, A. (2020) *The Wellness League Energy Top Up 5th April* https://www.youtube.com/watch?v=B6kbTcudtHA&t=44s (accessed 7 May 2020).

Index